YOU CAN
RECOVER, TOO!

Dr. Shannon Terrell Gordon

You Can Recover, Too!

Hello Reader,

Are you hurting because of the pain of a childhood spent emotionally alone?

Has someone you were supposed to be able to trust hurt you mentally, physically, or sexually?

Do you hunger for love and try to soothe your soul through romantic or sexual relationships that leave you empty?

Are you trapped in the web of darkness and insanity that goes along with alcohol or drug use and addiction?

Do you doubt whether a God exists because no one seems to be answering your prayers? Are you mad about that?

Does anxiety grip your chest and swirl your mind far more often than you'd like? Do you want your life to change but haven't the first clue how to make that happen? Are you in early recovery from any of that and feeling like you might shatter to bits? Do you want a better life but wonder if it's possible for you or just for other people? If so, then this book is for you!

May you find honesty, realism and hope in this – the life story of my triumphant, dearest friend with nearly 41 years of continuous sobriety and other recovery.

May the tools included in this book that helped her help you, too. You deserve your best life!

Shannon

PS: All of the people and events in this book are true. All names (including Bea's) – except for Wayside House treatment staff and current day friends of Bea's - have been changed to protect the innocent, and not-so-innocent!

You Can Recover, Too!

100% of the net proceeds of this book & resources will be donated to support recovery from complex trauma, anxiety, & substance use disorders.

You can make life better for yourself and others!

Dedication

To my bestie & my hero:

God used you to help save my life in its darkest season.

I'm trying to pay it forward so your ministry of recovery, redemption & hope continues.

To those who question whether life can be better:
YOU can recover too!

To Him who is able to do more than we can ask or even think…

Table of Contents

Dedication
1: Before Me
2: My Parents, My Family
3: My Grandparents
4: Double Reality Begins
5: Drinking & Trauma
6: Learning High Alert
7:More Mental Distortions, Enabling, Hidden
   Wounds, Blackouts, Makeup Gifts
8: Buster the Alcoholic
9: Childhood Fears & Realizations
10: I Wanted to Believe
11: Public Beating & First Runaway
12: My Brothers & Miss Toughie
13: Giving As Good As I Got
14: This is What You Need
15: Nana Really Loved Me
16: Loved Us the Best Way He Knew How
17: Good Student & A Mouth
18: Mr. Smelly
19: Formal Sex Education
20: Suspension Record
21: A Teacher Tried to Help
22: Rehab & the Heroin Addicts
23: My First
24:Parental Consent, the Cleaver & the Country
   Club
25: My Lover, His Wife, My Mom & My Foot
26: Cal, the Pipe Wrench & My Dad
27: High School Sweetheart
28: Relig
29: Effects on My Brother
30: College
31: Gang Rape

32: Florida & Dad's Demons Pick Up Speed

33: Protected Drinking & Tripping

34: Jon & the '57 Catalina

35: Drinking, Driving & Near Murder

36: Rationalizing Sex for Money & Abortion

37: Denial

38:Wedding Dress Hospital Lock Out & We're
    Going to Disney World

39: Married in Missouri

40: Living in My Pinto & Another Abortion

41: Mr. Smelly Had a Room for Rent, Boom

42: Ripped Off My Drug Dealer, Cancer & Cirrhosis

43: Stealing, Burying Bottles, Adding Water & AA

44: Grandma Cannon

45: The Wild Crowd, Paranoia, Darkness & Blood

46: A Bet, Cardiac Arrest, Evicted & Disowned

47: Holy Rollers to Detox

48: Too Far Gone for Wayside House for Women

49: Fear, Hallucinations & Anger

50: An Ex Con Fought for Me

51: Life at Wayside House

52: When AA Talked Abut God

53: Ed, Letters & Victim to Victor

54: Forgiveness & My First Prayer

55: Learning Right from Wrong Bit by Bit

56: Feelings? Rebellion & Anger Over Sadness

57: My Broken Picker & Return to Wayside

58: What Helped Me in Recovery

59: Broken Picker, Pregnant & Married Again

60: Amends & My Dad is Proud

61: Suicidal, Single Parenting & Adoption

62: Secrets Revealed, Looking for a Hit Man & a Gun

63: Therapy & Medication

64: Cancer, For Real

65: He Picked Up a Woman

66: Spiritual Seeking & Aliases

67: Moving

68: Dinner With My Brothers

69: Georgia Jobs

70: Still Seeking

71: A Different Kind of Church

72: New Life Outside a Closed Chick-Fil-A

73: The Couples Class & The Love of My Life

74: Living a Life of Joy & Service in Challenge

75: The Insidiousness of Addiction

76: Choose Well: You Are Worth It

A Letter of Love

Appendix 1: Important Questions You Might Consider

Appendix 2: Recovery Support Groups

Appendix 3: Simple Relaxation & Deep Breathing Practice

Appendix 4: Simple Mindfulness Practice

Appendix 5: Cognitive Behavioral Therapy Worksheets

Appendix 6: Scriptures that Have Helped Me Greatly

Epilogue

Celebrating Bea

Acknowledgements

About the Author

1: Before Me

During the era I was born, hospitals gave whiskey to premature infants. What a start to life, right?

Ireland's famine drove big and strapping James O'Brien to America at the turn of the twentieth century. Working his way over on a boat, he had absolutely nothing with him at arrival but his health and his dream of a better life.

Upon coming through Ellis Island and settling in New York state, he found the scourging ladder of prejudice alive and well in the U.S. of A. Over and over, "Irish need not apply" signs met him in the businesses where he sought work. He learned quickly that the Italians occupied the highest rung on the ladder of bigotry. Blacks were slightly lower. Irishmen like him were considered less than Blacks and only slightly above the Chinese.

Refusing to be denied his dream of a better life, he did what he had to do. He took grueling work laying railroad track alongside Chinese laborers. He saved his money.

Stern and strong, he soon met and married tiny Beatrice MacDougal, a petite immigrant from Scotland. They bought a home and settled in Binghamton, New York. James subsequently served as an infantryman in the Army during World War I, returning home with lung damage due to mustard gas exposure.

Together, James and Beatrice had three boys: Jim, John and Tom. As they built their family, James worked very hard. Bit by bit, he invested his earnings. Over time, he acquired rental houses, apartment buildings and restaurants. To manage his holdings, he formed a real estate company, James O'Brien and Sons.

In addition to being a hard-working businessman, James was cool and aloof, a stern disciplinarian to his boys. Today, he would be considered abusive for sure. As an example, when the boys misbehaved, James would sometimes hold them out a second floor window by their ankles to get their attention.

The years passed. The O'Brien sons grew into adulthood.

Even as adults, tiny Beatrice held her boys in check. When she spoke, it was "the law" to them, even after they were grown men.

Jim became a high-level police officer, even guarding the mayor of New York. John became a lawyer and went on to become a judge.

Youngest son Tom served in Korea as an Army jump master. Like his father, Tom was injured during his tour of duty. Tom broke his back when a parachute didn't open during a scheduled jump.

Upon returning home, Tom wanted to become an architect. However, James O'Brien changed the name of his company to James O'Brien and Son and looked to Tom to take over the family business.

Tom O'Brien was my father.

Gwen and George Cannon married and had four children: three girls and a boy. George loved and worked hard for their family. Gwen took care of their bustling brood of children and their picturesque home a pink house on Wellesley Island bounded by the St. Lawrence River. For some reason, I remember that the picture-perfect setting also had a storm cellar.

Their oldest child was a daughter, Lucy. Twin girls so identical no one but their mother could tell them apart came some time later: Pauline and Pearl. Their handsome, blonde, blue eyed son, Gordon, was the youngest. Pearl Cannon was my mother.

2: My Parents, My Family

I do not know how my parents met, but I know that they married while in their twenties. Oh, how my father loved my mother!

Entertaining and civic engagement was part of my dad's work in the real estate business. Also, he was an Elk, a member of the Lions Club and an usher at the local Catholic parish. He was incredibly well respected in the community. My mother was such a devout Catholic!

Even early in their marriage, though, my dad had a drinking problem. In response, my mom usually said a simple, placating, "Now, Tom " At times, however, my mom could get her Irish up and they would argue vehemently.

Unwittingly, my mother had been schooled in the family dynamics of alcoholism as she grew up. Though my Granddad Cannon was a hard-working and caring man, he was also an episodic, quiet alcoholic. My cousins told me that there were a few times of drunkenness and anger.

However, he was typically the type that, when he got a few too many drinks in him, would go to sleep with his head in his supper.

Unfortunately, my mom's dealing with alcoholism started early and carried on throughout her life. If only that had been the only thing she faced, her life would have been so much easier.

From the beginning, my father would walk through fire for my mother. As an example, my mom absolutely loved Christmas. Therefore, my dad would knock himself out with Christmas decorations.

Good Catholics that they were, my parents also started their family early. My oldest brother, Callahan Thomas, came quickly.

I am fourteen months younger than Cal, and my mom had a miscarriage between him and me.

I myself, Beatrice Mary O'Brien the middle child and only daughter of Tom and Pearl O'Brien was born when my mom was only six months pregnant. Weighing only pound and thirteen ounces at birth, I very nearly died. My incubator was an iron lung. All my life, I have had a habit of slightly rocking when I sit. My mom always said the slight rocking of the iron lung programmed the rock into me. My parents gave me whiskey to "keep my blood pumping." What foreshadowing of things to come!

My next brother, Finnegan James, was born nine months later. Then my brother, Liam, was born. Liam died of SIDS the day they were supposed to bring him home from the hospital.

Until I left home, we lived in this big, old house in a neighborhood of Binghamton, New York. All the neighbors Irish, German, Scottish and Black knew one another. Barbecues and parties were frequent.

I'll always remember the five steps to the landing with the stained-glass window in our house then ten more steps up to where my room was. My parents' room was across the hall from mine.

Because of where my room was, I had more of a bird's eye view of my parents' room. I remember the big thick board under their mattress that my dad used to help with his back pain that persisted after the war. Though he remained active throughout his life, back pain was his frequent companion.

I remember being able to hear, not the words of their conversations, but their tone and volume when they were downstairs and when they were in their bedroom with the door closed. That's how I knew when they would argue.

Down that hall and up a few more steps was the huge room that my two brothers shared.

My father did incredible work to fix up our house. He added a bathroom, a huge deck and screened porch, decking around our above ground pool, and redwood privacy fencing around our back yard.

He was very talented about things like that. I guess it was his handyman work that made him so strong.

From him, I got my work ethic, my patriotism and love of the good old U.S. of A.

My mom was a stereotypical mom of the 1950s. She kept a beautiful house, decorating it with many handmade crafts. She was a good cook and a wonderful seamstress.

I did not inherit her creative gifts! Truthfully, when I was a child and a teen, I thought all of that was hokey.

Over time, I came to understand that my mom really wanted to do right by us and loved us the best she knew how.

Though my mother was a very devout Catholic, Liam's death caused my parents' cooling with Catholic church doctrine.

After Liam died so mysteriously, the doctor told my mother that, if she had another child, she would die. My parents went to the church with that news.

The priest told them that, if they were true believers, even if it meant she died, they should do nothing to prevent pregnancy. God's will would be done. That day, my parents broke with the church, and my mother went on the pill.

By the time I was twelve, my father stopped going to church with us altogether.

I really loved my mother. In fact, my first memory is crying when I started kindergarten because I didn't want to leave her. I can see myself as a little girl standing by the fence crying.

Around that same time, though, was when I got my first bad beating.

3: My Grandparents

Though he was a stern disciplinarian, Grandad O'Brien did love us. I remember he'd give us cool things like 50 cent pieces and two-dollar bills. He'd take us for rides in his beloved, shiny black Cadillac covered in chrome with white interior. Man, we thought we were somebody when he would take us for a ride! To this day, in my mind's eye, I can see him riding with his signature unlit cigar hanging from his mouth.

My Grandmother O'Brien, I called her Nana, loved me. I knew it. She would tell me often. I loved it so much when she'd take me to Bloomingdale's for tea.

I also used to love to go to my see my mom's parents in the summer. The water was so beautiful, and their house was a house of peace and safety. Grandpa Cannon had a teak wooden boat that was his absolute pride and joy.

It was there I first started to love fishing Grandpa was so patient as he taught me. I remember we'd catch flounder and blow fish. I was fascinated with how they would expand.

My mother was a different person there. Weeks during the summer at my grandparents were peaceful. My father only come out on the weekends. His presence colored everything always.

4: Double Reality Begins

I used to love it when my parents entertained. It was the 1960s, and they had a lot of parties!

When people were at our house, it was safer. We could have fun and relax. But, any time we relaxed, something would happen, and all hell would break loose.

The night of my first bad beating, my parents were having a party at our house. I didn't do what my father thought I should. I was hanging on the guests, wanting too much attention, I guess.

Using just his tough fists, he beat my legs and my butt so bad that I couldn't bear for them to be touched for days.

I was no more than five years old. It was only the beginning.

My double reality had begun.

5: Drinking & Trauma

On the one hand, my father could be incredibly charming. He was very well respected in the community and civically minded. When he was at home, however, he was typically angry and withdrawn slamming things, kicking the dog, even kicking us. The addition of alcohol, however, always began a descent into more abuse.

There was that point, though, during each drinking episode before he got too drunk, where he was the life of the party. I would call him "Mr. Glad hand" then.

Sometimes, too, when he was drinking, he'd come home happy. He'd come in singing at two in the morning with White Castle hamburgers and hot chocolate. He'd wake us all up, and we'd eat burgers and hot chocolate in the middle of the night. That was crazy, but at least it was fun.

However, when he was the life of the party and you were "playing along" enjoying him, you never knew when he would turn on a dime to anger, accusing, "Why are you laughing?" or some such.

He nearly always held himself together when he drank in front of others. If he didn't, remember, times were different then. If you were stopped driving drunk back then, they didn't arrest you. They sent you home.

Also, remember, he owned half the town. One of his brothers was a high-ranking police officer. His other brother was an attorney or a judge in town. He had enough money and influence to make any instances go away where his temper or his drinking caused him any public trouble.

Many times, when he came home and had been drinking, he had a singular look in his eye. We would just know, "Somebody's going to get it tonight."

People saw our wealth and thought we were the perfect family. We were members of the country club. Our family walked in the Thanksgiving Day parade. We vacationed in Miami Beach. Publicly, my parents were cultured, though they did both smoke.

It was all about appearances. Then, there was our life at home.

For a long time, my dad was an episodic, functional alcoholic. But if he started drinking, it wasn't a question of *if* things would turn dark, it was a question of *when*.

As folks say, it's not about how much or how often you drink, it's about what happens when you do.

For my dad, when he started he couldn't stop, and what happened at the end of a drinking episode was never good.

I'm not talking about sloppiness, although he would drink until he was physically sick.

No, I'm talking about how it *always* ended in verbal and physical violence.

If he drank liquor, though, the violence escalated much earlier in the drinking episode. Something bad must have happened one time, because, at one point, my mom laid down the law, saying, "You can only drink beer." It was a family joke that he switched to beer to be less violent.

After that, he didn't drink liquor for a long time. Then he started with Crème de Menthe.

Even when he switched to beer, though, when he got super drunk, we'd hear about how he never had the chance to live his life because of the family business, because of us kids. He would frequently tell us all, but especially me, "I wish you had never been born."

My father was consumed by bitterness.

I think he likely had clinical depression, too. But back then, no one understood that or asked for help.

On top of that, he was so stern and had a billion rules in his mind that he never said out loud. But you certainly found out when an unspoken rule was broken, because he exploded all over anyone around.

Any little thing would set him off.

When I say "set him off," I don't mean he'd get irritated. I mean he could go from zero to ninety in three seconds. He'd start throwing things, breaking things, become a maniac!

You never knew what it was going to be. It could be breaking any one of his rules that mattered to him at the moment.

Did you put your elbow on the table? One night it wouldn't matter. Another night you'd get a beating. Did a friend call you on the phone? One night it wouldn't matter. Another night all hell would break loose.

I recall one particularly bad episode when I was ten or so. My mom made Christmas cookies and my brothers and I were in the kitchen having fun with her, taking a second to let our guard down to enjoy ourselves.

My dad came charging in the kitchen like a maniac, yelling, "You're crunching too loud! You're making too much noise!" He started throwing things everywhere! Crazy, right?

It was a weekly to daily occurrence.

You just never knew what was going to set him off. He was such an angry man, and he used that anger to discipline us. He was miserable, and we were the closest thing to spew it on.

Sometimes we were just being kids. He wanted to be left alone.

To me, it seemed that I was always doing the wrong thing at the wrong time, that I could never measure up.

The words he said to me were the *worst*: "You are a troublemaker." "You are more trouble than you are worth." "You are stupid." "You are a loser."

I think he knew his anger was over the top, but nobody got help back then. So, our double reality was learning to live a lie.

He'd throw a fit and hit us then say, "Get dressed. We're going to the country club."

We *knew* to maintain the pretense in public. We were the perfectly behaved, laughing, smiling happy family.

His business associates would come to the table and compliment him on being such great guy, and we'd all enthusiastically agree. God forbid if we didn't! He only hit me once in public. But, if any of us weren't *perfect*, just wait until we got home! There would be hell to pay in a beating. When I say a beating, I don't mean one smack. Sometimes, he'd only hit us two or three times. Sometimes, he couldn't stop. If he was being particularly brutal, my mother would interject, "Now, Tom ..." and he would ignore her.

What would make him stop?

Nobody knew.

6: Learning High Alert

I didn't understand then - or for many, many years after that - a child's brain develops best in relaxed, nurturing, predictable, sensory rich environments. I didn't understand that when a child grows up in an environment that is unpredictable, chaotic or scary, his or her developing brain literally adapts to live on high alert, far below the conscious level.

I didn't know, for years, that the "high alert" part of the brain is instinctual and part of our survival mechanism, the amygdala near the brain stem. I blamed myself for being "on alert" or nervous. In reality, my brain was adapting to my environment to try to survive.

7:
More Mental Distortions, Enabling, Hidden Wounds, Blackouts & Make Up Gifts

While we lived daily with the abuse, anger, fear, and never feeling safe or able to relax, there were other parts of life at home that added to the mental distortions.

There was my mom's way of justifying my dad's drinking and abuse. She'd say things like, "He didn't mean it," or "He was just tired." "You are just being oversensitive." "If you would just shut up." "If you would just be quiet. Don't egg him on. You make it worse." Man, that was so confusing.

Baloney. He was drunk. He was crazy.

She covered up for him for so many years. I would hear her lie for him, make excuses about why he couldn't go to a function so many times! The real reason? He was *drunk.*

Then, to add insult to injury, he was generally smart about where he hit us. Typically, my bruises were hidden on my butt, on my back or on my sides. He would not often hit me in the face. It was the same for my brothers.

To add to the feeling of insanity, there were the times when my dad would see marks or bruises, he had given me and would aggressively ask me, "What happened to you?"

I used to think he was lying, pretending, or that he was trying to make me feel crazy. I didn't know about blackouts in alcoholism until I started to have them.

Also, what I called his "make up gifts" added to the confusion. Sometimes, after a really bad blow up or a beating, he'd buy us gifts or things we really wanted, almost as a penance – though he never said he was sorry. As much as I liked the gifts, nothing was worth what I endured.

Distortion. Craziness. Our family's normal life.

8: Buster The Alcoholic

When I was five or six, we got Socks, the cat, as our first pet. A tabby with white feet, I never liked her. She scared me. She never forgave Buster, our Bassett hound, for joining the family about a year after her arrival. We got Buster as a puppy, and he was with us for 17 years.

Buster was my buddy.

When my parents would have parties, Buster would sniff the remnant glasses until he found ones with alcohol and drink them. I'll always remember him tripping drunkenly over his long floppy ears!

Even Buster was an alcoholic.

9: Childhood Fear & Realizations

As a child, I was incredibly scared of the dark. (Even into adulthood, I kept a light and TV on in the room as I slept.) When I was young, my parents thought I was being silly and I should get over it, so they wouldn't let me have a nightlight.

However, there was a lamp on a table on the stairs' landing. Light from it cast a beam onto my ceiling. I used to think that was God, and it comforted me.

My mother loved me as much as she could. Imagine being married to someone like that, watching your kids get beaten.

Though she witnessed so much abuse toward us, I came to feel sorry for my mom. She loved my dad and was, in many ways, trapped. She was from the generation that believed a wife should obey her husband in all things. She had no means of support until she went to work in the family business office when I was in late grammar school.

She wanted a girly girl, and she got me - a nervous kid who frustrated her.

Even after everything my dad did, there was a part of me that knew something was wrong with him.
Though I was mad at him, I felt sorry for him, too.

By second grade, anxiety and fear had become my constant friend. I guess you could say my brain was "well adapted" to our home's chaos.

10: I Wanted to Believe

By the time I was eight, I started praying every night that my parents would divorce or my dad would die. I wanted a way out of our life at home so badly! I started to think, "What kind of God is this? He's not helping us!"

Then, during the day, I was in Catholic school where the nuns reinforced talked about our going to hell and doing penance.

I wanted to believe in God so badly, but my concept of Him was terrible.

11: Public Beating &
First Run Away

The only time I ever got a beating in public was at church when I was eight or nine.

As you might imagine, I was a nervous wreck around my dad. This particular time, I wasn't trying to be disruptive, but I must have been wiggling or singing too loud or something.

My dad dragged me down the aisle and out the door.

Outside the church he started beating me with his fists, slapping me, punching me till I fell down on the ground. I was screaming bloody murder, but nobody ever came out. I don't remember anyone seeing me.

When I was ten, I ran away from home for the first time. I just thought, "I have got to get out of here. I have got to get away from these people. Anything's got to be better than this."

I don't remember how, but my parents brought me back home. Their response, "You don't know how good you've got it. You go to private school." But material things don't make a difference when your daily life is abuse.

I remember thinking, "I need to get smart about this running away thing. I need a better plan."

I couldn't go to a friend's house because their parents would call my parents, who would bring me back home. I couldn't go to the police because they were friends of my dad's.

So, I waited, and I endured.

As the years of abuse rolled on, the hurt and anger built like gunpowder in a bomb.

12: My Brothers & Miss Toughie

My brothers were "all boy" and typical brothers. They played together and fought together. Somebody was always knocking a hole in the wall or injuring the other one in their scuffles. I remember one time our neighbor was spreading grass seed and, somehow, one brother put a pitchfork through the foot of the other! It seemed we were always heading to the hospital for stitches.

They teased me unmercifully and called me "Miss Toughie" because I was such a scrapper. Though I was little, I could beat up nearly any boy in the neighborhood.

13: Giving As Good As I Got

Scrappy is also how I handled my dad's abuse. When younger, my brothers used to run and hide when we'd hear the change in his steps or the change in his voice.

When he'd pull in the driveway, they'd run. I wouldn't.

I figured if I was going to get a beating anyway, I was going to go down swinging. I would never hit back physically, but I would try to give it to him verbally. My father *hated* to hear a girl swear, and I would use ever swear word I knew and some I made up! I also would never let him see me cry no matter what. I was his target, and I was going to do my best to give as good as I got.

Finn would withdraw or be sick, even as a teen. To this day, he is brilliant but flakey, living in his own world.

As he moved into adolescence, Cal got more angry, more arrogant, more dad-like, but not as mean. He would fight my dad when he was a teenager. I always felt like Cal had my back.

Dad very, very rarely hit my mother. The few times he did, she would respond with her, "Now, Tom" and wouldn't speak to him for days. That is, of course, except for the episode when my brother Cal was seventeen, but more about that later.

14: This Is What You Need

Though I don't remember my mom drinking when I was young, everything in our house revolved around alcohol. When I was five or six, my dad started giving me sips of his mixed drinks saying, "This is what you need. This will keep you from being so (whatever)." It did. It took away the fear. It helped me relax.

When I was eight or nine, I started stealing drinks. By the time I was ten I was drinking for the effect. I also started stealing whatever I could find out of the medicine cabinet. Sometimes it took away my feelings. Sometimes it was Exlax!

As a part of my dad's business dealings, people would try to earn favors by giving him cases of booze. He stored it in the hall closet with the winter coats.

As a small child, I started to steal it. My parents never missed it.

15: Nana Really Loved Me

I really feel like my Nana O'Brien was the only one in my family who really loved me.

I will always remember that, one time when we were visiting when I was five or six, I told her that my dad beat me. As little as she was, she beat the crap out of my dad. I liked that a lot! He didn't touch me for a while. That was a relief!

In addition to our tea parties at Bloomingdale's, another funny thing I liked about Nana O'Brien was that she smoked cigarettes, though Granddad didn't want her to. I always laugh when I remember seeing her toss her lit cigarette into a desk drawer when she heard him coming up the stone front steps of their house. I thought she was going to burn the house down!

My Nana O'Brien died of a heart attack when I was ten. It was my first experience with death.

Typical for the way my family communicated, nobody would tell us kids what was going on until the funeral. I don't remember the wake at all. In my family, a wake was just an excuse for everyone to get snockered anyway.

I was absolutely stunned. I remember thinking, "What is going to happen to me now?" I don't remember if I cried. By then, I had learned to turn off my feelings to survive.

Nana O'Brien's death is the only time I ever saw my dad cry. He was positively undone. My granddad was broken, too. He never remarried.

I handled it by just going on like nothing happened. It's what I had learned.

To this day, I am not sure if what I am about to tell you really happened or if I dreamed it. It was so real!

I had the experience of Nana O'Brien coming to me one night after she died. She reassured me that everything was going to be alright. For some reason, I told my parents the next morning.

My dad became absolutely unhinged. He said it was not real, demonic. He beat the crap out of me with his fists because of what I said.

He was so strong.

16: Loved Us the Best Way He Knew How

During the days of my childhood, I attended private, Catholic grammar school. Back then, there was no junior high or middle school. Grammar school went through the eighth grade.

I liked learning, but I didn't always like the nuns. The ones with high standards who really believed in you were fine. The ones who were stern and unpleasable, not so much.

Back in those days, people were superstitious. When I started trying to write with my left hand in first grade, the nuns tied my left hand behind my back to force me to write with my right hand.

Somehow, my father heard about it. He went to the school and raised a really big stink. They never did that again.

It's things like that that make me think, today, that he loved us the best way he knew how.

17: Good Student & a Mouth

Though I was a good student throughout all my school years, by second grade I was a holy terror. From a young age, I had trouble controlling my mouth. I would question the nuns, especially what they said about God. I would argue with them.

The anger had started to build. After all, I had all this stuff going on at home that I didn't know what to do with. It poured out in the way I acted. I started forming an identity as a hellion and a scrapper.

My least favorite teacher was in fourth grade. She had this folding yard stick, and she made misbehaving students like me turn our hands over so that she could hit the bones and knuckles. It really hurt. I'll always remember that.

18: Mr. Smelly

So, age ten was not only the year Nana O'Brien died, but it was the year I had my least favorite teacher, and the year I started to clean houses in the neighborhood for money.

I was friends with this kid across the street. His parents weren't together. Sometime later, his dad moved up the street from us. His dad was on old smelly guy, and he said he'd let me clean his house.

When I went to do the work, he started sexually abusing me. He told me I had to come back. I was a kid. I believed him.

To say the least, it was not a good year.

He abused me at least every other week for two years. I never told a soul. I felt like if I told my parents they wouldn't believe me. My brother, Cal, was off doing his own thing by then.

When I got to be about twelve, I realized I did not have to do what "Old Mr. Smelly" said. I told him I was never coming back to clean his house, and I never did.

Thankfully, we never had intercourse. There's more to that story, but I'll get to it later.

19: Formal Sex Education

I started my period the year I turned twelve. I came home from a game of "cream the ball carrier" and was bleeding. I thought I was injured! I told my mom.

My sex education? She gave me a sanitary belt, a box of pads and a pamphlet. She didn't think tampons were proper.

20: Suspension Record

As I was finishing eighth grade, I really, really wanted to go to the public high school. That's where the boys and the partying were.

My parents said, "Not just no, but $#%& no!"

They made me go to an all-girls, Catholic high school.

My double life of keeping up appearances while living through violence and destruction was in full swing. I had learned it well.

On the one hand I was the girl who went to private school, attended classes and made good grades.

On the other hand, many days, as soon as my dad dropped me off at school and drove away, I was on the corner hanging with the boys, smoking and doing drugs.

The nuns didn't know what to do with me.

I had the record for being suspended more times than anyone in the history of the school. Every time I got in trouble, my dad would make another big donation to the school so they wouldn't kick me out. One of my friends jokes that my high school education is the only one ever that cost a quarter of a million dollars!

A dear friend recently asked me, since my behavior was so out of control for so many years, if anyone ever offered to talk to me or asked me to tell them about my hurt? Never. Never.

21: A Teacher Tried to Help

By the time I was fourteen, I had mellowed some. By then, I would only fight if someone backed me in a corner. Most of my fights were sticking up for someone who was being picked on. But, I was heavily into drugs.

When I was a freshman, my algebra teacher caught me selling drugs at school. Not just pot pills and acid, too.

She knew I was a person who never really wanted to hurt anyone. She had a couple of friends who were chemically dependent who went to a rehab center in a nearby town. When she confronted me, she said, "I want you to go there."

Eyes wide as saucers, I quickly said, "My parents would never agree."

She said, "I'm not asking you. I'm telling you. Go there. Participate in the outpatient program six months, and I won't tell your parents or the school." That sounded like a good deal to me!

I know she was trying to do right by me, to save me. Little did she know she was opening the floodgates of hell for me, a fourteen- year old girl.

22: Rehab & the Heroin Addicts

At the rehab center, my drinking really took off. Though most members of the rehab center were heroin addicts, the culture was that if we didn't do heroin, it was okay.

For the most part, they liked me, tried to look out for me, and keep me from killing myself by doing any drug at any time and mixing alcohol with drugs.

They would never let me use needles or do heroin. Using crystal meth was okay. I thought I was so grown up.

Very soon after I started there, I met my first lover: a 24-year-old, married heroin addict.

23: My First

All I really wanted was to be loved. This relationship began a repetitive pattern of looking for love in all the wrong places for many, many years. Swept off my feet as a fourteen-year-old by my first motorcycle ride, we had sex for the first time in his marital bed.

I was so naïve. I did not know that virgins often bleed during their first intercourse. I bled all over the sheets.

To this day, in my mind's eye, I can see him slicing his thumb with a razor so that there would be a plausible explanation for the blood on the sheets.

Growing up, the nuns had told us repeatedly that, if we masturbated or had sex, an "A" would appear on our foreheads. I *completely* believed them. The day after we first had sex, I was incredibly shocked that my mother showed no reaction when I went home. I vividly remember going into the bathroom, lifting my bangs and searching for the mark.

The married heroin addict and I were together for several years. I remember that my brother Cal got in a fist fight with him because he didn't want me going out with him. I also vividly remember that, when I was 17, he introduced me to meth.

24:
Parental Consent, the Cleaver & the Country Club

Backing up a bit: After some time at the drug facility, staff came to me and said I had to get at least one parent's consent.

At the time, my father was out of town on a business trip, also known as "geting drunk with the boys". In my irrational logic, I took one of the heroin addicts home to explain it to my mother. Picture a grown man with long hair with chains and earrings wearing motorcycle leathers explaining to an upper middle class Irish Catholic mother why it is a good idea for her teenage daughter to participate in a drug program with him.

My mother threw him out of the house! Dragging me in tow, she marched to the drug rehab facility. She told them, in no uncertain terms, that I was underage. With her Irish *way* up, she told them that she would press charges and make sure they were shut down if they ever let me come again.

Then, she dragged me home.

I remember sitting on the bar stool at the counter in our kitchen while we continued to argue. Both of us were crying. She was going on and on about, "People can't know about this! What will the neighbors think?" I got the message I was grounded until I was at least 106!

About that time, my dad came home. He'd obviously been drinking.

He takes one look at me, does not say one word or ask one question. Boom! He hits me so hard he knocks me off the stool and thunders, "You're pregnant!"

My mother screams hysterically, "No, Tom! It's worse! She's a drug addict!"

In that instant, my father came from together to apart. He went absolutely crazy. He lunged on top of me and began slamming my head against the floor.

I remember thinking, "I'm not the crazy one. You people are nuts certifiable." I kept trying to get up. He kept hitting me.

At some point, my brother Cal came into the room. My father had my brother hold me down so he could continue to hit me as my mother sobbed in the background. (Cal's philosophy regarding handling my dad was, "Just shut up.") Then, I remember this stillness.

In the most sinister voice I'd ever heard him use my father said, "I ought to kill you."

Bucking and screaming like a banshee, I screamed, "Good. Take me out so I can get out of this crazy family. Kill me please! You'd be doing me a favor! But you're going to look me dead in the eye when you do it."

He grabbed a butcher knife out of the block on the counter, put it up against my throat and hissed, "I'm going to kill you. I'm going to kill you dead."

All the while I am yelling, "Do it! Do it! Do it! Here's Mr. Cleaver for you. He's got a cleaver and it's up against my throat. That's why they call him Mr. Cleaver!"

That's the only time I remember, during a beating, hearing my mother quietly say, "Tom, stop."

For some reason, he listened to her. He suddenly threw the knife to the side and bellowed, "We're going to have court! You are guilty! You're a drug addict, and you're going to jail!"

I remember thinking, "Hmmmm, okay, this is different!"

He dragged me up to my room. He took every stitch of clothing out of the room and made me strip to my underwear. For dramatic effect, he brought a bowl of bread and a bowl of water. He went to the hardware store and bought a hasp and padlock, and installed them on my door.

He pronounced with flourish, "This is your sentence," and he locked me in.

I didn't care. I had bottles of liquor hidden in my drop ceiling, so I got drunk!

I don't remember how long I was in there. At some point, though, he decided my sentence was over. He came in like nothing ever happened saying, "Get dressed. We're going to the country club for dinner." My face was so bruised and puffy from his beating that I looked like I'd been through a war.

At the country club, no one ever said a word.

Times were different then. I would like to think, today, someone would intervene. Back then, I was the only one who talked.

People have asked me if I was mad at Cal for holding me down that day. I was mad at everybody, but really no madder at Cal. Though Cal, Finn and I never talked about it, we all understood our house was one of survival. Everybody understood it was every person for themselves against the old man.

25:
My Lover, His Wife, My Mom & My Foot

Shortly after, I got the bright idea I was going to take the train to a nearby town. As I was walking down the road, I remember taking off my sandals because they hurt my feet. I remember my bare feet on the pavement.

As I was walking, I ran into my married lover and his wife bless her soul. She didn't know about the affair, and she liked me.

About that time, I saw my mom coming in her red Firebird, so I took off running through an overgrown field.

As I was running, I stepped on something. It came up and nearly cut my foot completely in half. The only thing holding my foot on my body was the skin on the top of my foot. My lover had been following me as I ran. He hurriedly got a garbage bag from somewhere, put my leg in it, and physically carried me to the car. They took me to the hospital.

I had tons and tons of stitches that day, and I was on crutches almost a year.

After that day, I didn't see the married heroin addict for several years. I don't remember why it ended, whether because he went to jail or his wife got pregnant.

26: Cal, The Pipe Wrench & My Dad

However, I do remember that during the time I was on crutches when I was 15, my father came home drunk with that look in his eye. I don't think Finn was home that day.

For some reason, Dad's anger was focused on my mother. He began to beat her in the kitchen.

Seventeen-year-old Cal stepped in, "You are *not* going to hit my mother. You are *NOT* going to hit my mother."

My dad turned on Cal, and the two of them started fighting. At seventeen, Cal was stronger than my dad.

Until then, Cal had responded to my dad's aggression only by shoving him back.

That day, I really don't know how a pipe wrench entered the picture, but Cal hit my dad across the mouth with a pipe wrench.

It was one of those moments in which time stood still.

In an instant, I heard a cracking sound as my father's jaw broke. My dad's lip was suddenly blown apart. There was blood and there were teeth *everywhere*. It looked like something out of a movie.

In my mind, I shouted, "Yes! Finally! Somebody got you!" but I didn't utter a sound. Somebody called an ambulance. My dad was taken to the hospital.

At some point in the hullaballoo, Cal was arrested.

However, at some point, Cal must have said, "You really want to do this? It will ruin that Cleaver image."

My dad dropped the charges.

As a result of all the scarring from that incident, my dad had to wear a mustache and a beard until the day he died.

It was also around that time that Finn fell off the loading dock at one of my dad's apartment buildings. He fractured his skull and started having seizures.

Things were quiet at home for a while after that. As soon as I got off crutches, I ran away again.

27: High School Sweetheart

When I was a sophomore, I started dating Paul Pietra as my high school sweetheart. I don't really remember how we met. Maybe he was a friend of my brother? I thought he was cool and really liked him.

He drank beer, but he didn't drink like an alcoholic. I was still using and drinking a lot. He had no awareness of that.

What I was aware of was that he was crazy about me. That's what I wanted.

He was good to me, treated me really well. He was my date to both my junior and senior proms. He really loved me, as much as a teenager could.

That, to me, was like a first. I had desperately been looking for someone to love me all my life.

That's all I ever wanted, you know? Though I had been with the married guy for years, I knew I wasn't special to him.

There was always a part of me that wanted bright things. Coexisting with that part were the voices in my head learned through my childhood, "You are not good enough." "If they really knew you, they wouldn't accept you."

I lived in a constant war of thoughts and emotions. I wanted something different and didn't have a clue how to get it.

At that time, in my mind, I wasn't unfaithful to Paul through the relationship with the married guy. And in my screwed up logic, I wasn't doing anything wrong by sleeping with a married man because I wasn't the one who was married. Oh, the repercussions of so much practice living simultaneous realities!

28: Relig

By this time it is the early 1970s.

It was also around that time that my brother Cal got involved in a club called Relig at his high school, the public high school in Binghamton. He had been expelled from a private Catholic school for fighting.

This really cool man named John Dean was in charge of Relig. He was humble, and he just wanted to reach the kids for Christ. Though I never thought of him as young, John Dean must have been a young man then. He is elderly now, and he and I are friends on Facebook today.

Though I was still drinking and using, I started going to Relig, too. There was part of me that wanted bright and good things, too. I was just never sure it would be possible.

Around that same time, my brother Cal grew his hair really long. He and my dad argued all the time about it. I remember Cal had this poster in his room of Christ. The caption said, "Just tell them I said you can wear your hair as long as you want." Now an accountant, Cal had long hair until just a few years ago.

I kept going to Relig until I graduated from high school.

29: Effects on My Brother

Cal, who was 14 months older than me, graduated from high school and went into the Marines. His fighting ways continued, and he spent many a day in the brig for it while he was in the service.

30: College

After graduation, I enrolled at CW Post College, a division of private Long Island University. I either majored in criminal justice with a minor in psychology or vice versa. I can't remember.

I don't remember because, by the time I went to college, addiction had me deep in its clutches. By this point, I was using drugs to avoid withdrawal. I also was completely convinced that, if I stopped drinking and using, I would shatter into a million pieces.

I broke up with sweet, kind Paul when I went off to college to focus on partying. Paul became another one of addiction's innocent casualties. I still have a soft spot in my heart for him.

My time in college was a disaster because there was no restraint on me whatsoever. Drugs were everywhere. As soon as I turned 18, I could drink, too! By my late teens I was drinking up to three quarts of vodka a day, unwittingly financed by my parents.

Amazingly, until I decided to drop out to focus on partying, I miraculously maintained a 3.0 GPA. Though I hardly ever went to class and rarely studied, I have my transcript to prove it!

My roommate in college was Carole Anne Watson. CW, I called her, was as beautiful as a model and was dating the student body president, Ben Goldman. Though Ben looked the part of a hippie, he didn't do drugs, was a nice guy and was in a fraternity.

He was crazy about CW, though they later broke up after she got hooked on drugs.

Man, folks in our dorm used to hate it when we would go on adventures. We'd leave Jefferson Airplane playing loudly on the record player on repeat so we could find our way back to the dorm when we were high!

One night, CW and I were doing chocolate mescaline, a lightweight psychedelic. She was twirling like a ballerina to make the visual trails, and I got the bright idea that I could fly. I told her matter-of-factly that I was going to fly to the other building across the quad and got up on the ledge of our third floor dorm room window to take off. She and Ben yanked me down.

In my addiction, I couldn't recognize God at the time. Most of the time, however, He had people around me who protected me from myself a break of sun through the clouds. Little did I know at the time that the clouds were going to get much darker.

31: Gang Rape

Another night during my freshman year, a guy named Aaron Greenbaum invited me to go with him to a party in Hampstead. I was already drunk, so, though I did not know him from Adam's housecat, I agreed to go with him. Why? Because there were supposed to be drugs there.

To this day, I swear somebody put something in my drink after we arrived.

The next thing I know, I wake up on a bed in a bedroom I had never seen. A guy is on top of me banging away on me. Around the bed were four to six guys loudly laughing, clapping, and cheering him on.

After he finished raping me, they all took turns. It was horrible. I was humiliated.

When they were finished with me and I was putting on my clothes, Aaron says, "Don't you tell anybody."

I remember fighting with Aaron about taking me back to campus. At first he didn't want to, but he finally did.

I am glad I was so wasted because I only remember snatches of it.

Though nothing ever justifies a person being raped, it's a fact that when a person is willing to go anywhere for drugs, ending up unintended places and situations is a consequence.

When I arrived back at the college, I was sick from the drugs I had taken and the drinking I had done. I was emotionally distraught, too.

I told CW and Ben what happened.

Either that night or the next day, Ben called his friend Tiny – a huge, giant of a guy. Ben, Tiny and several of Ben's fraternity brothers ambushed Aaron when he returned to campus. Tiny pulled a fence post out of the ground. He and the other guys beat him so badly they broke his leg and nearly killed him.

Ben told me their parting words to him were, "Now you be the one who don't tell nobody, or we will make you pay."

No charges were ever filed.

I wasn't going to go public. There was stigma, especially back then: "You did something to deserve it."

It wasn't really fear about what my family would have thought. I was far enough away from family that they wouldn't have heard.

I never got medical care or counseling, and that was incredibly rough.

People have asked me if that happening contributed to my deciding to drop out of college. Consciously, it did not. However, I was the queen of compartmentalizing back then.

One of the greatest regrets of my life is how I wasted college. Grandpa O'Brien paid for it. All I had to do was show up and finish. But I didn't. I dropped out to make more time for partying. The day I dropped out, my parents told me they disowned me.

32:

Florida & Dad's Demons Pick Up Speed

After Finn graduated from high school, my parents left New York and moved to Florida initially to Pompano Beach.

My dad's drinking really picked up once they got there.

So, they bought a hotel: *Beach Cove on the Ocean* in Boynton Beach.

33: Protected Drinking & Tripping

Meanwhile, back in New York, I got a job bartending at a place called Flo's Bar where all the police officers hung out. I liked it a lot. I made money. I could drink on the job. Having police officers as customers kept me from being arrested for DWI or driving without a license. I hadn't gotten a license because I was afraid, I wouldn't pass the test.

In addition to drinking, I did a lot of chocolate mescaline, too. I could drink it when cut up small and put in Nestle's Quick. I could only eat happy trails and peyote button mushrooms, other more strong psychedelics, in a ketchup sandwich. They would make me sick before sending me off on a trip. Orange barrel and purple microdot LSD were also drugs I used during that period.

My using buddies during that time were Rick Baker and his roommate Jonathan Bush from Hoboken, New Jersey. I'll always remember that Jonathan looked like an Eskimo in his fluffy down coat. Those two guys and Derrick, a tall very skinny Black guy with a huge afro, dropped acid with me all the time.

I will always remember the last time I used acid. We had been tripping for about three days, and I got a feeling it was going to be a bad trip when we went to Schaeffer Jazz Festival in Central Park.

Police were everywhere. People were pressing in. I told Jeff, "I gotta get out of here." But, if we left, we would not be allowed to return.

As the trip continued, I remember being so scared. I couldn't control anything and was hallucinating nonstop. I remember lying on the ground, that I could only look at sky. Across my field of vision were all these devils.

I remember praying, "God, if you let me come off this acid trip in one piece with my mind in one piece, I'll never do acid again." And I never did.

Shortly after that, Rick was tripping and couldn't come down. He had a psychotic break and thought he was a cat. He almost bit me, and he bit Jon on the face! We had to call the paramedics, and they had to take him away in a straitjacket to a mental hospital. I remember the craziest things from my life. For example, one of the most memorable parts of that experience was that he was so mad because his sneakers were stolen there.

34: Jon & the '57 Catalina

As I have mentioned before, part of the way I established my worthiness at that time was having a man in my life. Rick and Jon were part of that history, too.

I initially was dating Rick. However, I thought Jon was cuter. Over time, I migrated to him and he and I came to live in a multi apartment house together. It wasn't exactly like a commune, but close.

Though Jon smoked hash and pot, he didn't do hard drugs and underneath the partying lifestyle we shared he was a basically nice guy. Too, he had the most beautiful brown metallic '57 Catalina that was his absolute pride and joy.

As much as I was capable at the time, we cared about each other. I even met his parents. Since he was Jewish, his mom kept saying, "Jonathan, you can't marry a shiksa girl!"

I was going to convert to Judaism until I found out how much work it was to be a practicing Jew! I have a few pretty significant memories from when I was in a relationship with Jonathan.

One night, I was coming home from working a shift at Flo's Bar around three in the morning. Though I had been doing THC, I was driving his beloved Catalina. I began to have an out of body experience and lost control of the car.

The next thing I knew, I crashed into a telephone pole. The telephone pole snapped in half and smashed a garbage can at its base to smithereens.

When I came to my stoned senses, I was lying flat on the grass, having been ejected from the car. Loose electrical wires were snapping and crackling in the air. Suddenly, a lady in a bathrobe and curlers was standing over me screeching, "Are you going to pay for my garbage can?"

I thought, "I gotta get out of here." I started crawling across the grass on my hands and knees toward the completely totaled car.

One of my bar buddy cops was the first officer on the scene.

He kept saying to me, "Shut up, and get in the car. Don't say a word."

For once in my life, I listened to someone and was quiet. I didn't want to go to jail. Oh my, Jon was mad about his beloved Catalina.

35: Drinking, Driving & Near Murder

More times than I can count, during that and subsequent seasons, I would be so drunk I would crawl to my car on my hands and knees. I would then get behind the wheel and drive. Amazingly, I never got a DUI, never had another wreck, and never hurt anyone else in a car. God was looking out for me, even though I couldn't see it.

Not too long after the Catalina incident, Jon said a dealer had some drugs he'd let us have on credit to sell. He let me go to get them, though he knew the dealer had the hots for me.

I went. The dealer and I got to partying, and I didn't come home for three days. I don't think the dealer and I slept together, but I honestly don't remember. We were so high.

I came home, and Jon came unglued. He grabbed me by the throat. As he started choking me, he started banging my head on the metal frame of the sofa bed we slept on.

All I can tell you is that something inside me snapped.

I swore the day I left my father's house that no one was ever going to hit me again, and I remember thinking very clearly, "I'm going to kill you!"

I somehow got away from Jonathan and ran into the kitchen. I grabbed a butcher knife and started straight for his heart.

God's grace intervened.

At the last second, he threw his arm up. I cut him from his shoulder to his elbow. He was severely injured.

His blood starting to pour forth doused my white hot fury. I realized what I had done, and I ran. I ran, and I ran.

Eventually, I ended up at my neighbor's upstairs apartment.

Jon obviously had to have medical care, but he didn't call the police. Though I was bruised and beaten, I didn't seek medical care.

When he got home from the hospital, I went back downstairs. We just looked at each other, both so shell-shocked like, "What the hell just happened?"

It was so sad.

I simply said, "I can't stay." I knew the relationship was over.

That episode scared me so badly. I had never done anything like that before, and I've never laid a hand on anybody since.

In retrospect, I realize that the abuse I had lived through in my past influenced the intensity of my reaction that day. Isn't reacting from past pain how people derail their lives so many times?

I was 18 years old. My future was preserved only by God's grace.

2

36:
Rationalizing Sex for Money & Abortion

After the break up with Jonathan, I rented a room from some drinking buddies from the bar. I was sleeping with a bunch of guys. I would even sleep with men occasionally for money. My philosophy, "I've slept with enough men. Why not make some money when I need it?" It is amazing what we can rationalize in our own minds. As I have heard it said, we should not believe everything we think!

As can happen when that's your lifestyle, I got pregnant. My strategy at that time: If I ignore it, I'll go away. Time passed. And more time passed.

I had maintained my friendship with Rhoda Moore, a buddy of Jon's. Her boyfriend was in the Air Force, and he was assigned to a base in Abilene, Texas. She said, "Why don't you move out here with us?" So I did.

After I moved there, I waitressed to with Rhoda at Testa's Italian Restaurant.

Rhoda went with me as I had a late-term abortion. I remember thinking, as soon as it was over, "Oh my God, I just killed a baby."

Like I did with everything else in my life, I shut off my feelings to try to survive. I went on with my life.

37: Denial

Again, I picked up dating a series of guys. I was looking for love, and free love was a part of the drinking and drugging lifestyle. In my crazy thinking, as long as I had a guy on my arm, I was okay.

In truth, though I had so many issues, I was with good guys. Yes, they drank, but they did not drink alcoholically.

My denial- fueled philosophy was, "If I can get you to have one drink, I can have twelve."

When people hear the term "denial," they often think it's a conscious choice. It's not. It's not like I thought, "I realize I have a problem with alcohol, but I am going to pretend I don't." Denial is as unconscious a process as a heartbeat. When the truth or emotions seem too overwhelming to face, the human mind rationalizes it with a story that manages the overwhelming feelings.

38:
Wedding Dress
Hospital Lock Out.
We're Going to Disney World!

Soon after I turned 19, I met Patrick Keegan, who was 23 and also in the Air Force in Abilene. He was a nice guy.

I knew I didn't like what I was doing, and I wanted somebody to love me just me for me.

He told me he loved me and that he wanted to get married. I thought, "Why not?"

When I broke the silence with my parents to tell them I was getting married, my father's first words were "Ah, a nice Irish boy." My parents were thrilled. They thought marriage was just what I needed to settle me down.

My parents were insistent that we marry at the hotel they owned in Florida. When we got engaged, little did I know that I would meet him in Texas, marry him in Florida and end up living with him in Missouri.

While we were planning the wedding, it was coming time for Patrick to get orders for his overseas placement. He really wanted to go to Italy. When his orders came, they were for Germany. He was not happy.

Back then, though, if you decided you wanted to get out of the military, you could just tell them you smoked pot. That admission would deem you "psychologically unfit," and they would give you an *honorable* discharge. So, our plan after our wedding and honeymoon was to return to Patrick's tiny hometown in Missouri to live.

As my wedding day approached, I started to feel bad. I didn't think I really loved him. I knew I was such a screw up. I was drinking and doing drugs heavily. In truth, I was a garbage head. I would take anything to get me high. Knowing that, I wanted to back out. My parents were having none of it, however.

The day of the wedding, my parents locked me in one of the hotel rooms to make sure I would make it to the wedding. In the hotel room with me, however, was a keg of beer. I had a good time with that keg that day. By the time of the ceremony, I was so drunk that my father half-carried me up the aisle.

Believe it or not, the story gets even more bizarre.

My brother, Finnegan, drank at the reception and began having seizures. The entire wedding party ended up at the nearby emergency room.

Finn was so upset, feeling like he had ruined my wedding. I was upset because I did not think the nurses were being as attentive as I thought they should be. I didn't care about disrupting the wedding, as long as they took care of my baby brother.

I went toe-to-toe with one of the nurses about it. I was so disruptive that they locked me out of the hospital. I can still picture myself in my wedding dress banging on the glass of the hospital door.

Amazingly, as he was driving me back to the hotel, my father told me he was proud of me for standing up for my brother. I remember his exact words, "I'm proud of you. You did good girl!"

It was one of the few times in my life he ever told me he was proud of me – because, when advocating for my brother, I had raised such a stink they banned me from the hospital. Insanity continued.

Guess where Patrick and I went on our honeymoon? Disney World. Somehow poetically fitting, right?

39: Married in Missouri

After the wedding and honeymoon, Patrick and I went to live in Missouri in a little house on his parents' multi-acre property. His parents were nice people, and he had a brother named Tim who was six years younger than he was. When we married, Patrick was 23, I was 19, and Tim was 17. At first, his parents loved me. Then, they got to know me.

At his parents' house was the first time I ever had homemade wine. Wow! That stuff was like corn liquor. One jelly glass of the concoction and I was wasted! They thought it was hilarious.

Drinking and drugs, especially meth, were prevalent in that small town. While Patrick was in school and working as a tool and die maker, I had a number of jobs over the three years we were together. I would work my shift then party with friends.

One of the jobs I had was at Captain D's. I worked there for one day. The manager and I agreed I was not cut out for the fast food industry, especially anything involving fish.

Then I worked as an aide in a nursing home. I found that too heartbreaking and depressing.

After that, I worked the night shift alone at The Learning Center, a place that was known back then as for the "educable mentally retarded." Oh, how times were different then!

One of my most memorable patients was Beth, a 17 year old girl who had absolutely nothing wrong with her except cerebral palsy. I loved her!

Another, Mia, was blind and beat the crap out of me on a regular basis.

Most could not have conversations, and my job was to teach them to dress themselves. In my off time, I was drinking and drugging with people around town.

I hid what I could from Patrick, but he knew enough to know I was partying hard. At first, Patrick didn't say much about my behavior. Over time, however, he started to speak up about not drinking so much or not drinking so early. Needless to say, I didn't care for that one bit!

While we were together, my drug habits progressed to the point that I would go into Patrick's parents' house when they weren't home and take his dad's prescription Valium.

Though they loved me when they met me, once his parents got to know me, they didn't like me. I don't blame them. Back then, I didn't like me either.

The breaking point for our unhealthy relationship? One night, while partying with Patrick's younger brother's friends, I slept with one of them.

Amazingly, Patrick didn't leave me, even then. I left him. I thought I was a scumbag, and I couldn't stay with anybody who wanted to stay with me.

40: Living in My Pinto & Another Abortion

When I left Patrick, I drove from Missouri across the country back to New York in my white Ford Pinto. I wanted to see if I could live there again. For at least the first year back there, I slept in my car. I had a sleeping bag and a pillow that fit over the emergency brake to enhance my comfort! They came to repossess my car once because I hadn't been making payments. I talked them out of it somehow.

During this time, I was in sporadic contact with my brothers. Finnegan was on crutches for some reason, and I dismissed him as a hypochondriac. Cal gave me grief about drinking and drugging so much. How did they know how much I was using?

All they had to do was look at me. I had reached the point in my addiction that I didn't go anywhere or do anything unless I was wasted, and I was sick *all* the time.

So why didn't I stop? Mentally, I was completely convinced that using was the only thing that was keeping me from the nuthouse. I genuinely believed that, if I stopped, I would shatter into a million pieces. Too, if I went more than a few hours without a drink, I started getting the shakes, though I did not understand that was physical withdrawal from alcohol.

As was my way back then, I convinced myself that if I could get a man, I was okay.

After I returned to New York, for a while I worked at the pizza parlor where I had worked in high school. I also had a job as a telemarketer. I was good at it, for I was often cranked out of my mind. Folks would give in and buy from me just to get me off the phone!

Living that way, in relatively short order, I got pregnant by one of my bosses at the telemarketing company. This time, I did not deny or procrastinate. He paid for the abortion, and I had it quickly.

41: Mr. Smelly Had a Room for Rent. Boom!

While back in New York, I also responded to a newspaper ad for a room. When I went to see it, the homeowner was "Old Mr. Smelly!" He remembered me and thought we'd just pick up where he left off. I thought, "I'll get you sucker." I accepted the room.

I wanted him dead, but I didn't want to kill him because I did not want to go to jail or hell.

In a moment of rare clarity in those days, I soon thought, "What are you doing? Get your stuff and get out of here!"

When I went to get my things, he wouldn't give them to me. I was so mad!

Wasted, I told one of my using buddies, a heavy-set man whose mom was a high-ranking police officer in town, about my situation. In our drug-fogged logic, we decided we were going to burn up Old Mr. Smelly's car. My friend lit it, and we ran like bats out of hell.

When the fire lit the gas tank, the car exploded! The force of the blast was so strong it busted all the windows out of Old Mr. Smelly's house and the house next door.

My first thought? "I got you sucker. I hope this made you poop your pants." My companion's slurred first words? "My mom is going to be really mad."

His mother questioned us both, and we were adamant that we knew nothing, saw nothing, did nothing. She let us go. Again, God was merciful to me.

42: Ripped Off my Drug Dealer, Cancer & Cirrhosis

By then, I was routinely doing meth. One day, I badly needed money, so I decided to rip off my drug dealer. I stole drugs and cash. He shot at me as I was leaving. The bullet broke out the passenger side window.

I thought, "If I stay in New York, these guys are going to kill me. I'm going to die." I also thought, since the window was broken out of my car, "Oh, it's too cold. I gotta go to Florida."

I needed money to get there, so I called my mom and convinced her I had cancer. I told her I needed $500 to get to Florida. She sent it.

I used most of the money for drugs. Then I took off for Florida.

Using addict logic, I would do all these crazy things, and then say, "I didn't do it on purpose. I didn't know that was going to happen."

When I got to Florida, my parents immediately took me to the doctor. The doctor said, "You don't have cancer. You have the beginnings of cirrhosis of the liver. If you don't quit drinking, you'll be dead in five years."

I looked at him, serious as a heart attack and believing it with every fiber of my being in that moment and responded, "That's impossible! I only drink a six-pack a week."

Like I said, you don't believe you are lying when your life is a lie.

In relatively short order, the repo man caught up with me. They repossessed my Pinto.

43:
Stealing, Burying Bottles, Adding Water & AA

I guess my parents thought they had to do something with me, so they told me I could work for them at the hotel. Since I didn't have a car, I could only work when someone took me. It wasn't long before I was stealing from the guests.

I was 22 years old.

I had bottles everywhere: buried in sand on the beach and in laundry carts. My parents started marking their bottles at home. When I got desperate enough for a drink, I would run in the house and act like I was going to the bathroom. I would run to the liquor cabinet, drink, run to the kitchen to fill up the bottle to the line, then run to put it back to liquor cabinet.
One time, my Dad was sitting on the couch in the living room watching me do this insane routine in a reflection of mirrors on the wall.

Prior to that day, they had said, "You just can't drink liquor." So, I'd drink a gallon of wine instead.
Whew that gave me terrible hangovers!

That day, my dad said, "You have an alcohol problem. You need to go to AA." I made my mother go with me, and I thought it was a bunch of crap!

Amazingly, though I was the girl who didn't care if anyone saw me crawling down the street on my hands and knees because I was so drunk I could not walk, I did not want anyone to see me going into "those meetings." I felt embarrassed.

I went, but I wasn't ready to stop drinking. Exposure to the fact that alcoholics could stop drinking did help till the soil of my heart for days to come, however.

44: Grandma Cannon

Around that same time, my mother's mother, Grandma Cannon, developed Alzheimer's and started deteriorating mentally. By then, my granddad had died. The siblings argued about who was going to be responsible for her care, and somehow my mother became responsible. My mother went to New York and picked her up.

Back then, there were no assisted living facilities, so my parents put my grandmother and me up in a condominium to live together.

It was a little weird living with Grandma Cannon, given her mental decline. However, she didn't say anything about my drinking!

She allotted herself to drink a six-pack of beer a week. This worked out to almost a beer a day for her – unless, of course, I miscalculated my own use. Back then, what was mine was mine, and what was hers was mine, too.

45: The Wild Crowd, Paranoia, Darkness & Blood

Since my car had been repossessed, I could work only if my parents or someone picked me up. Grandma and I didn't live near the beach either. However, somehow. I still hooked up with the wild crowd.

Wherever you go, there you are, you know?

People with motorcycles were my "crowd." They were frequent visitors. I was often openly drunk and disorderly in the driveway or at the neighborhood pool.

By this point, I was heavily drinking and doing methamphetamines. As a result, my paranoia had become so extreme that I most often only went out at night. What a metaphor for the darkness my life had become!

However, in my soggy logic, I figured if I couldn't see you, you couldn't see me. The shadows of "I gotta get that next drink, next drug" robbed all the colors from my life.

Physically, I continued to be sick all the time. Though it had been happening for a while, I had gotten used to throwing up and pooping fresh, red blood. My belly was so distended, I looked like I was going to give birth.

The people who lived next door to Grandma Cannon and me were the "holy roller" type of Christians. They were absolutely convinced they could get me straight. They would ask to pray for me, and I would let them. And I kept drinking and drugging.

46: A Bet, Cardiac Arrest, Evicted & Disowned

Around this same time I started dating a guy named Dennis. He worked, and he was a dealer. By this point, I had gotten so deep into my addiction that I was robbing him blind drugs, cash, anything that wasn't nailed down.

When he found out, his response was, "You gotta quit doing drugs, but you can still drink."

When his things kept "walking off," he said, "I'll bet you a thousand dollars you can't quit drinking for thirty days."

Since I completely believed that I did not have a problem with alcohol, I took him up on his bet.

Within hours, I started having severe shakes as my body began the process of physical withdrawal from alcohol.

I thought, "Okay, I gotta get out of the house to cope." So, I walked down to the pool. Once I arrived at the pool area, I started seizing.

I have been told that, during the seizure, I lost consciousness and fell into the water. The people who were at the pool at the time initially assumed I was just drunk again, as I had been to the pool soused so many times before.

However, when they saw me start floating face down, they pulled me out of the water to the pool deck. I am so grateful!

I immediately began seizing again, so someone called the paramedics.

Soon after the paramedics arrived and loaded me onto the gurney, I stopped breathing and went into cardiac arrest. Using the paddles to shock my heart, the paramedics revived me.

When I regained consciousness, I saw the paramedics hovering over me holding the electric paddles and thought, "These people are trying to kill me!"

Totally terrified, I jumped off the gurney and took off running. My only thought was to get away.

Imagine the sight: a crazed 23 year old running madly in soaking wet street clothes!

When the paramedics caught me, I flatly refused to go with them because, in my paranoid state, I was sure they would take me to jail.

My behavior during that episode was the last straw for the management of the complex. They evicted my grandmother and me. My parents were so mad! They became responsible for the daily care of my grandmother, who had become a real handful by then.

My parents disowned me that day again.

47: Holy Rollers to Detox

As I was adamantly refusing to go with the paramedics, my next-door neighbors, the holy rollers who had been praying over me, arrived. They convinced me, "You gotta go somewhere. We will take you." Since they had tried to help me before and I thought they were nice people, I agreed to go with them.

Bless them, they took me to a suicide center, even though I wasn't suicidal.

The suicide center staff told them I needed detox. So, my neighbors loaded soggy me up again and took me to the community detox center.

The detox center was in this old, run down house. Detox centers back then were very different than detox centers today. I arrived as the only woman.

When they admitted me, they gave me a bag to vomit in and a spoon wrapped in a napkin to keep in my mouth if I started having seizures. Since I was the only female, they assigned me to a room by myself. The room contained only a cot.

Oh my, I was so sick! As withdrawal began, I started felling a crawling sensation all over my legs and arms, the "whiskey fleas" that are a common part of unmanaged alcohol withdrawal. As the delirium tremens progressed, I started having hallucinations.

Because I did not understand that delirium tremens are a consequence of untreated alcohol withdrawal, I thought, "See I'm cracking up and losing it just like I thought I would!"

Though I was certain I was going insane, the heart attack had scared me bad enough to make me stay. Also, remember my car had been repossessed. I had been evicted, and my parents had disowned me. Sometimes difficult circumstances can be great motivators for change!

Even now, though, detoxification services are intended to be only short term, just to stabilize a person physically. Often, people go to either outpatient or residential treatment after detox to help them learn how to live in recovery.

48:

Too Far Gone for Wayside House for Women

In the town at that time there was a residential addiction treatment program for women called Wayside House for Women. The director was a lady named Phyllis Michelfelder. Ms. Michelfelder came to the detox unit to staff my case toward considering me for admission to Wayside House.

I eavesdropped outside the door of the room where they were holding the case conference. I could hear them talking about me. She didn't want to take me. I heard her say, "It sounds like she is too far gone."

Man, that got my Irish up! That's the best way to motivate me: tell me I can't do it.

God, in His mercy and grace, changed her mind. She let me go from detox to Wayside House. How grateful I am that finances weren't a consideration for Wayside House at that time. I didn't have a penny to my name, and no one in my family would have helped with the cost of treatment.

49: Fear Hallucinations & Anger

Upon my arrival at Wayside House, I was still one sick cookie. I wasn't the model patient who is just so grateful to in be in treatment. I was *not* grateful to be there! Initially, though, the heart attack scared me bad enough to make me stay.

I wouldn't stay in my bedroom because I kept having visual hallucinations of arms coming out of the closet trying to pull me inside. I kept seeing things under the bed, too. Terrified to be alone in my private room, I stayed on the couch in the living room.

To say I was incredibly anxious was the understatement of the century.

I could not sleep for days on end. The first time I finally did fall asleep, I had a cigarette in my hand and burned my shoulder badly.

Though they became less frequent over time, my hallucinations lasted for months. Finally, they stopped all together. I was and am so grateful.

In addition to seeing things and being filled with fear, I had such an anger problem! I wanted to fight with everybody. I was "anti" everything "just because." Everybody was scared of me. I was scared of me!

50: An Ex-Con Fought for Me

Given that the hallucinations persisted for months and given that I was so anxious and angry, Phyllis Michelfelder wanted to put me in the psychiatric ward. One man fought for me, though. His name was Ed Kelley.

Ed Kelley was my assigned counselor. He was this huge Black guy in recovery from heroin addiction after serving time in Raiford Prison in Florida. He had my number right away. Every time someone would say I was too far gone, he would stand up for me.

Many times I heard him remind people, "Her biggest problem is that she started using so early. That's causing all these other problems." He really fought for me, and I wasn't used to anyone fighting for me.

When I would hallucinate, Ed would say, "It will get better. You only have to do this once."

When I would shake with fear, Ed would say, "It will get better. You only have to do this once."

When I would throw a fit of anger, Ed would say, "It will get better. You only have to do this once."

For some unknown reason, I chose to believe him. I am so grateful.

Ed's believing in me, Ed's fighting for me, Ed's pushing me to get in touch with my feelings, and Ed's simply encouraging me saved my life.

I say again: ex-con Ed Kelley saved my life.

51: Life at Wayside House

Life at Wayside House was structured and predictable. We got up at a standard time each morning. We had time to get ready and to take care of our personal area. We each had assigned chores and a schedule to help prepare meals.

The treatment services at Wayside House were simple. Daily group counseling and three meetings a day of Alcoholics Anonymous. Back then Narcotics Anonymous was not nearly as available as it is today. We were required to get and work with a sponsor.

Too, Ed would give me writing assignments. He had me write out my history several times. He had me write letters to significant others in my life. Today, I understand that the purpose of those assignments was to help me get in touch with what my life had really been and what my choices had really caused for myself and for others.

It really shocked me that many I had considered my "ride or die" friends from my old life disappeared when I started trying to get sober. I learned quickly that they didn't want anything to do with me if I wasn't using.

Dennis, the guy I had been dating who bet me a thousand dollars I couldn't quit drinking, came to get me for my first pass at Wayside House. He was allowed to take me out to lunch. Guess where he took me? To a bar. His rationale? "You can drink. Just don't do drugs."

By the time of my first pass, though, I had been to enough AA meetings for it to have penetrated my still soggy brain that, perhaps, that wasn't the best idea. Truthfully, wanting to stay sober wasn't the reason I didn't drink that day. I didn't drink because was scared of my heart stopping again if I used. I knew I didn't want to die.

Thankfully, I made it back from my pass without drinking. Dennis didn't come to visit me again.

Life was regimented at Wayside House, and participation was not optional. Actually, it *was* optional, I suppose. We could opt to do it, or they would opt for us to leave!

I am not kidding when I say that nothing was optional. For example, one day before an AA dance, my roommate, Jonni, offered to dye my hair, making it as platinum as hers. My hair came out rusty orange, but I still had to go to that dance!

Let me be clear, again, that I was not a model patient. After decades of abuse, defiance and use, I did not have the first clue about how to follow rules or be compliant. I complained. I whined. I cried. I pitched more than my share of fits. How grateful I am, however, that they "watched my feet." Though I complained, cried and whined, I followed the schedule and did the assignments. I did what they said, so they let me stay.

Please understand, there were many, many times I would *say*, "F#@* this! I'm leaving!" But then I would stay.

Why? Fighting was what I knew, so that was my first reaction.

At the same time, I knew I didn't want to die. While I was in treatment, I was terrified that, if I used again, I would die.

Then, there was a part of me that wanted something different, though I wasn't sure that different could really be true for *me*. The longer I stayed in recovery, the part of me that wanted a better life and believed it could be possible grew teensy bit by teensy bit. There is no such thing as microwave recovery!

The daily pattern of life at Wayside House was helpful to help me to begin to restructure what had been the chaos of my life. After all, at that time, what did I know about what I needed? What did I know about thinking healthy thoughts or living a healthy and responsible life? Absolutely nothing.

Since I knew nothing about what I needed to recover, how grateful I am that I had people in my life who, when I would defiantly announce, "This is what I'm going to do" had enough strength to respond with, "No you are not! This is what you need to do." They would stay after me until I did it. After all, my best decisions had led to the shambles my life had become.

Living in a house full of women shed light on areas I needed to work on in my relationships. For example, others having expectations of me helped expose my issues with authority, defiance and anger.

As I have subsequently learned, situations and circumstances do not cause me to think, feel or behave a certain way, they expose my internal life and coping skills. I am grateful for all Wayside exposed in me and taught me.

Here I was not even liking women living in a house with more than twenty women. Every day at Wayside we would have this group where the twenty women would rate each other on whether we thought each other would stay sober. Every day, I came in last. That fired up my Irish stubbornness to prove all their predictions wrong.

The seeds of determination started to germinate. Ed told us that in ten or fifteen years only two of the twenty of us would still be sober. I made up my mind that I would be one of them. I am so grateful to be alive and sober today.

I am also so grateful that my time in Wayside House helped me move from not even liking women to learning to have friendships with them. Too, I began to learn to foster friendships for the right reasons: relationships, recovery and realness.

52: When AA Talked About God

Back then, when we would go to AA meetings, if anybody even mentioned God, I would get so mad! Remember, I had the emotions of the little girl who was so disappointed with God because she had prayed for years for relief from the abuse.

I would jump to my feet, point my finger around the room and challenge them loudly, "You're all weak. God is nothing but a crutch. Don't even bother talking about Him. He doesn't do nothing!"

I was beyond disrespectful.

Folks in the group would just patiently pat me and say, "Don't drink, don't take any drugs, and come back tomorrow."

God was so merciful to me. I am so grateful that God meets us where we are with grace and mercy.

I would not be sober today were it not for the patience and tough love from the "winners" in the rooms of AA and NA back then.

53: Ed, Letters &
Victim to Victor

Back at Wayside House, in counseling, Ed and I talked a lot about how mad I was at my dad. Ed also helped me realize that as mad as I was at my dad I was madder at my mother. On some level, I knew that my dad was mentally ill. That didn't excuse his behavior, but it gave me at least a smidgen of compassion for him. However, my mother was sane but did nothing to protect her children from his tyranny.

Therefore, my letters to significant others turned out to be letters to my parents.

Though Ed was gentle with me as he encouraged me about how I would only have to do this once, he would also push me – really hard - when it would help me in recovery.

He had me write my story *over* and *over* and *over*. At first, I left out details because my brain and thinking were still soggy and unclear. Then, shame was the gatekeeper of my memories of what had been done to me and all the ways I had been so selfish, dishonest and hurtful. Too, I had so many unconscious defense mechanisms around the chasm of my heart, which was so full of pain.

At the time, I thought it was totally and completely ridiculous that he had me re-write my story so many times. Today, I understand he was persistently, gently helping me connect my mind to reality, helping me penetrate layer upon layer of the unconscious lies that had become my life.

My thinking was so distorted I thought I deserved all that had happened to me and that I was justified in all I had done. I minimized the amount of my use and its consequences.

Little by little, Ed and I talked about all the ways I was victimized as a child by my father and "Old Mr. Smelly," and by the college students who raped me.

After he helped me honor all of that, he began to gently introduce the idea that for my own sake I had to consciously choose to move from a victim to victor. At first, I resisted incredibly. He just didn't understand!

"I am this way because this happened to me! It's all their fault," I would loudly protest.

However, over time I began to see he was right. No matter what has happened in our pasts, at some point, if we are going to be successful, we have to come to the point of saying, "That happened to me, but I will not let it define my present and my future.

I cannot blame anyone or anything for the choices I made in the past or the choices I make from today forward. I must take personal responsibility."

Honestly? I had to start from the place of, "The best revenge is a happy life." Revenge as a motive is something I understood at the time.

54:

Forgiveness & My First Prayer

Next, Ed challenged that, if I wanted freedom, I had to forgive my abusers. Initially, I rebelled about the concept of forgiveness. As Ed won me over because he was the only one in my life, other than Grandma

O'Brien, who had ever fought for me my prayers toward forgiving my dad began with, "Dear God, please help me not hate that son of a bitch so bad!"

For me at least, like all other aspects of my recovery and growth, forgiveness has been a slow process over time like peeling a reeking onion! I shed many, many tears over days, months, and years.

As I said, I am so grateful that God meets us where we are with grace and mercy. God was so merciful to me to tolerate my awful, unholy attitudes. He has been so merciful with me to give me the gifts of forgiveness toward those who have wounded me. The hardest person to forgive? Myself. I struggled to forgive myself for how I wounded others and for how I hurt myself.

55:
Learning Right from Wrong Bit by Bit

As I also said, I was *not* the model patient during the first six months I was at Wayside House.

The chip on my shoulder was the size of a boulder. I walked around simultaneously expecting someone to knock it off and daring them to do so. People were afraid of my temper and I was, too!

Coming off meth was so hard; I was so paranoid! I was as anxious as a long-tailed cat in a room full of rocking chairs, and I chain-smoked to try to cope.

Fbombs were a part of nearly every sentence I spoke. I truly did not know right from wrong.

Here's an example: Some days, a group of Wayside House residents would walk to a nearby Eckerd's drug store. Once, while there, I saw a pair of sunglasses I liked, so I stole them.

As we were walking back, one of the other women commented about my sunglasses and asked where I got them.

"Eckerd's," I said.

"But you don't have any money," she said.

"Eh..." I responded, shrugging my shoulders nonchalantly, as we continued to walk.

"Stealing is *wrong*," my co-resident told me.

"Really?" I responded; my blue eyes wide as saucers with shock. Truly, I had been doing whatever I wanted to do however I wanted to do it for so many years that hearing that stealing was wrong surprised me out of my shoes! Prior to this day, I had rationalized stealing as okay because I needed or wanted something.

"Okay. I won't do it again," I said sheepishly.

That is just one tiny example of the hundreds of ways I had to learn to think differently, to speak differently and to act differently to achieve and maintain a life of sobriety.

56:

Feelings?
Rebellion & Anger Over Sadness

During the time that I was in treatment, the hallucinations got farther apart and less intense. That is not to say that I felt comfortable in my own skin. I did not, for a very long time. It took years actually. Especially early in recovery, as my brain cleared and I worked with Ed and with the group, emotions started coming up. It is no exaggeration to say I did not know what they were or where they came from. I had numbed for so long that I was completely out of touch with my mind and heart.

The predominant emotion I felt was anger. I had a serious, serious anger problem, a hair trigger temper. I rebelled against *everything*. I would fight anybody about anything at any time. But the people in the 12 step meetings were so incredibly patient with me. No matter how many swear words I would hurl or how I would show out, they would patiently not react and just say, "Don't drink or use, and come back tomorrow."

People have asked me about the source of my anger. I really don't know exactly. I think underneath the anger was incredible sadness about not feeling a part of anything, always seeming to do the wrong thing and being asked to leave.

Therefore, somewhere in my mind, I was challenging, "Are you going to love me now? Are you going to stick with me now?" No matter how hard I tried to push them away, they wouldn't let me.

In retrospect, I know that my rebellious spirit made my journey so much harder for me than it had to be.

However, while at Wayside House, there also began to be short periods when I felt okay. When those brief respites would come, please understand I did not grab them and run with them, work hard to enlarge them or even know that I could. Rather, my experience was more, "Hmmm, that's interesting." Still, I was changing bit by bit.

Like I said, three 12 step meetings a day and getting a sponsor was life at Wayside House. My sponsor would tell me things to do to help me, and I would say, "I'm not going to do that!" but then I would. I went to meetings, often being the first one there. I got involved in service by making coffee and cleaning up. We would go out for coffee after meetings. I would do what my sponsor told me.

I had such a persisting desire to use. She would tell me to go to a meeting, tell the group I wanted to use, and ask for feedback. I hated doing that! But, I did it.

Some feedback that helped me: "Don't think about staying sober one day at a time; think about one minute at a time."

I read Alcoholics Anonymous' *The Big Book* and *Twenty-four Hours a Day* over and over, talked about it with my sponsor, and tried to put into practice what I was reading.

I wrote gratitude lists. I journaled. I called people in the program who would talk to me no matter what time of day it was.

I helped newcomers. This helped me realize that, though it might not seem as if I had come very far in my recovery, life was so much better for me now that I wasn't using.

2

57:
My Broken Picker
& Return to Wayside

Another example of my poor attitude and nearly nonexistent listening skills back then?

We were repeatedly told that we should avoid a relationship with the opposite sex until we had a year of sobriety. What did I do? I became emotionally involved with a man named Matthew Fitzpatrick who was also early in seeking recovery.

After six months at Wayside House, I left treatment because I was "in love." Matthew and I moved in together. He worked as a painter, and I worked as a telephone solicitor.

In summary, I was crazy, and he was crazier. It wasn't until later that I came to understand that he had paranoid schizophrenia and was a raging alcoholic.

That was my way back then. Line up all the guys, and pick the one who was the most screwed up. My "picker" was broken nearly beyond repair!

Neither of us knew how to be responsible or pay bills. We got evicted in short order.

Even through that turbulent time, I did not drink or use.

When we were evicted, I really had nowhere else to go. I asked to return to Wayside House. I knew I needed to learn better skills to live, and I promised to do *anything* they asked of me.

Graciously, they let me return and I stayed three more months. The focus of those three months was living life outside of treatment. Get a job. Get up to go to a job even when I don't like it or I don't feel like it. Work eight hours for eight hours of pay. Don't quit a job until you have another one. Learn to manage money. Learn to pay bills. Learn to have fun sober. Wayside House started to teach me how to live a responsible life as an adult.

Another evidence of God's grace: Remember Phyllis Michelfelder, the woman who initially said I was too far gone to be helped? After I established recovery, Phyllis and I went on to become friends.

She was an amazing woman.

58: What Helped Me In Recovery

People have asked me about my experience in recovery. What helped me? Early on, the fear of dying if I used again helped me. After all, my heart had already stopped once!

The structure and firm expectations of Wayside House helped me. People being willing to teach me right from wrong helped me.

So much exposure to Alcoholics Anonymous and the twelve steps helped me. I went to at least two meetings a day for two years. Hearing and hearing and hearing recovery language until it became my thoughts and words helped me. Over and over I heard things like, "Stick with the winners." "Do the work." "Easy Does It." "Just for Today." Repetitive exposure to recovery concepts helped me. Working the steps over and over and over helped me.

Working with a sponsor helped me. Building friendships with sober people helped me. I have a friend who says, "That Lone Ranger s*^% don't work." That is so true, especially when trying to build a life of recovery!

In summary, learning by *doing* is what helped me most. Please understand that it was only by doing these things over and over and over and over and over that I began to change bit by bit. And bit by bit is the *truth*. There is no microwave change of character and recovery. If I had it to do over again, I would know to celebrate every tiny change.

Make no mistake about it: The mind has to change. I had to replace unhealthy thoughts with healthier ones. Concretely, I have learned to say to myself, "When I have an anxious thought, I will replace it with a good thought instead."

At the same time, learning mental concepts without behavioral action changes nothing. Like it is said in recovery, "When nothing changes, nothing changes." "Talk is cheap. Watch the feet."

Simple things helped me, too. As a tiny example of hundreds, my sponsor told me to start wearing my watch on the other arm. At first I thought she was crazy. What was the point of that? Today I realize that those instructions from my sponsor helped me learn to be willing to take direction from others rather than always having my way. She helped me learn to do things differently.

Though I have neither slipped or relapsed since my last drink on March 30, 1981, that is not to say that the desire to use left me quickly. The desire to drink or use stayed with me for *years*. However, my sponsor taught me to say, "If this doesn't work for me, I can use tomorrow."

Thankfully, "tomorrow" has not yet come.

There seems to be a growing line of thinking these days that relapses are inevitable because addiction is a chronic illness. Hear me: I am living proof you do not have to relapse! Choosing to drink or use is playing Russian roulette for an addict like me. I know *many* who have died in their relapse.

Anyway, where fear of dying kept me from using for a long time, little by little the blackness of active using that had robbed all light from my life started to lift. I can remember sitting on the steps of Wayside House smoking a cigarette and noticing the simple things of a sunshiny day and the flowers blooming. Being able to see and notice those few tiny glimpses of brightness were some of the first seedlings of hope for me.

After having been told all my life, "You're not worth anything and nothing but a loser and a screw-up," I started to believe, "Maybe I can do this."

Over time, the hope that a good life could be mine began to take hold in my bruised heart. I shifted from *having* to stay clean to keep from dying to *wanting* to stay clean to have a better life. Those were the beginnings of my made-up mind that, "No matter what happens, I am *not* going to pick up a drink or a drug to cope with life!" When I started to have hope for myself, my motivation for recovery shifted from the shaky foundation of fear to the bedrock of determination to protect my recovery as a foundational building block of my life. Again, inch by inch and bit by bit.

I often say that a life of recovery is not built with one or two big choices but many small decisions to do things differently. I often refer to it as a tapestry, woven one thread at a time.

The fear of dying did scare me. However, the longer I stayed sober, the more I realized there are worse things than dying. What is worse? Living in the chains of addiction, having no real friends other than users, and having no hope. I was winning freedom inch by inch. I was building friendships better than I'd ever had. Hope was building in me. I worked hard to protect every inch of ground I gained.

59:

Broken Picker, Pregnant & Married Again

After I left Wayside the second time, Matthew and I broke up and got back together a bunch. Then, of course, I got pregnant.

I knew I couldn't have an abortion sober, so Matthew and I got married.

Given our openly rocky relationship, *everybody* we knew was telling us not to get married. Did I listen? Consistent with my lifestyle back then, of course not. As was predicted, things stayed stormy between us. God sent one redemption for Matthew and I in September 1982, when Christina Michelle Fitzpatrick was born.

After Christina was born, Matthew and I continued our pattern of together and apart many times.

In my immature logic, I thought, "Another kid will fix the problems in our relationship." Purposefully, I got pregnant.

Not surprisingly, throughout the pregnancy, the tumult in our relationship continued. Again, however, God sent a beautiful baby as a ray of sunshine. In February 1984, Brooke O'Brien Fitzpatrick was born.

Matthew and I split permanently shortly after Brooke was born. I took my beautiful girls, then 2 and about 6 months old, and left.

Initially, Matthew visited the girls, and I would let them go with him to visit his family in Michigan. However, as soon as I could get the money together, I formally divorced him.

60: Amends & My Dad is Proud

As I worked the steps of AA, I contacted my parents to make amends. When I arrived back in Florida with the girls, we began to visit them sporadically, too.

A memory from that time: When I celebrated five years of sobriety, my dad gave me a card that said he was proud of me. That was pretty amazing.

61: Suicidal, Single Parenting & Adoption

As you know, having a man in my life was a huge validator for me. All my life, I have just wanted to be loved.

I met Don F. in AA. He was 16 years older than me, and we developed a relationship. We were crazy about each other, and he introduced me to the Fifth Chapter Motorcycle Club. All members of Fifth Chapter are people in recovery from alcoholism or addiction and following the tenets outlined by Alcoholics

Anonymous. The name "Fifth Chapter" references the fifth chapter of the AA Big Book, "How it Works." Don was supportive of me and the girls. However, though we were in a relationship, most of the childcare fell to me.

Life as, essentially, a single parent of two young children is not for sissies. I was working two jobs trying to keep the bills paid and the household running with the basics.

I ran a day care during the day, and I had a second job as a phone solicitor in the evenings. I had been good at phone sales when I was high on crank back in the day. When I was sober, man how I hated that job! I stayed at it though, because I had learned in Wayside House not to leave until I had found another job.

Even working two jobs, I was just barely able to pay the bills. I tried really hard to take care of my girls with nearly no outside help. Over time, I got so very tired.

I started to feel totally overwhelmed and exhausted. I barely saw my girls. It seemed I was swimming as hard as I could and barely treading water.

I started having suicidal thoughts. Even then, I did not drink or use. For that, I am so grateful.

Too, over time, I became increasingly terrified of Christina and Brooke being around my father. It wasn't that he ever hurt them physically, I just didn't want them to be around his toxic thinking. I became obsessed with his not contaminating them when they visited.

I wanted my girls to have a normal life with a present mom, a healthy dad, a house, a yard, and a dog. These were things I knew I could not give them, no matter how hard I tried.

Therefore, I started talking to my AA sponsor about placing the girls for adoption. After months of agonizing, I finally decided to pursue open adoption through Catholic Social Services.

Brooke was 3 and a half. Christina was 5.

When I told my mother and father that I was placing them for adoption, my dad freaked!

He said, "They're not puppies. You don't just decide you don't like them anymore and give them away!"

I remained adamant, "I want them to have a better life than what I can give them."

His response? "If you do that, you are dead to us. It will be like you have never been born, like you don't exist."

I simply said, "Well, whatever you gotta do."

I looked at my mom and questioned, "Is this how you feel?"

She responded, "I stand with my husband."

I said, "I understand now," and left. Strangely, their rejection didn't seem to affect me all that much. After all, it was really nothing different than what I experienced all my years of growing up.

Some things never change. But I was changing.

Years later, my cousin Kathy told me that her mother, my mother's twin sister, Pat, would come back from visiting my mom after that all torn up. Aunt Pat reported trying to talk about me to my mom and my mom responding, "We are not allowed to talk about that."

Aunt Pat and cousin Kathy believe in closeness of family, so my parents' responses were alien to them. Somehow, knowing that comforts me to this day.

The judgment and criticism I faced about my decision, unfortunately, was not limited to my father. Though Don was supportive, I was attacked and cussed out by friends, by people in AA. I was a pariah to so many. Please understand that I do not believe that somebody disagreeing means they are hurtful. Many were, however, *hurtful*.

I didn't care.

My attitude was, "You can do whatever you want to me. You can kill me. I don't care. I want my kids to have a better life."

The adoption and peoples' reactions was beyond agonizing, but I never wavered in my resolve to give my children the best possible chance for a good life.

As a part of the adoption process, the agency told me I could write letters to each of the girls. I did. The caseworker told me they were some of the most beautiful letters she had ever read. That comforted me, too.

I was told that the girls were adopted together into a well to do home. Initially, I was allowed to call the agency to get reports about them once a month.

Emotionally, it was horrible for me. To survive, I did what I had learned to do so well. I shut off that compartment of my heart as best I could and went on with my life.

62:
Secrets Revealed, Looking for a Hit Man & a Gun

Shortly after they were adopted, one of the girls started acting out sexually. Their new parents followed up quickly, and the girls disclosed that their father, Matthew, had been sexually abusing them during his visits. He had told them, "If you tell your mother, I'm going to hurt her." They stayed quiet to protect me!

Thank God, they got into an environment where they felt safe enough to tell someone!

Their new parents immediately got them into counseling. It was reported to me that, with intervention so early, the effects on them would be much lessened. It was explained to me that, to a young child, the behaviors aren't sexual. It's to the adult that it's sexual behavior.

Though I did not pick up a drink or a drug when I learned of Matthew's violation of my precious girls, I fell completely apart mentally and emotionally.

I had a friend in AA who used to be in the Mafia. I called him and asked him to help me take out a contract to have Matthew killed.

My friend wouldn't do it saying, "You don't want that on your conscience." "Oh yes, I do! Yes, I do!" was my response.

He remained firm denying my request.

When he wouldn't do what I wanted, I decided I would kill Matthew myself.

At that time, I was running with the Fifth Chapter Motorcycle Club. I tried to get a gun. No matter how I tried, I couldn't get one.

Again, the hand of God intervened to save me from myself.

Though I had already lived through so much, that almost killed me. My heart hurt so badly, I thought I would die.

Thankfully, Matthew was tried, convicted and sent to prison.

I just kept repeating in my mind, "My girls are safe. He doesn't know where they are. He can't get to them. He can't find them. They can have a good life." That was all the comfort I could find about that horrific discovery.

Then, to add insult to injury, about a year after the adoption, Catholic Social Services told me I couldn't call for reports anymore. They said, "You have to let it go."

That was the last straw. To therapy I went, a shattered mess.

63: Therapy & Medication

I learned a lot in therapy that has proven helpful to me through the years.

I learned that the anxiety that had plagued me since childhood even into recovery had its roots in growing up in a "walking on eggshells don't know what is going to set him off" house of abuse. The counselor told me I might always have a hyper alert antenna about the atmosphere of situations. It was a survival skill ingrained in my childhood.

My counselor taught me some important skills to help manage the anxiety, like breathing deeply in through my nose and out through my mouth. Too, he taught me, when my thoughts began to race, to focus my mind on my body position feet on the floor, back in the chair, etc. Both of those things still help me to this day.

He worked with me on cognitive behavioral therapy, changing my thinking. He taught me that our thinking propels us forward or backward. He taught me to dissect my thinking when I felt anxious feelings:

- What is the activating event?
- What is my initial belief about that event?
- What are my emotional consequences based on that initial belief?

- What evidence exists to dispute my initial belief?
- What evidence exists to dispute my initial emotions?

(See Appendix 1 for a therapy template..)

I filled journal after journal as I practiced slowing myself down and "grabbing my thoughts." It gave me more peace than I had ever had. Again, I "did the work" really hard work for an extended period and was greatly helped.

However, even with all his and all my effort and the fact that things *were* better, anxiety remained a near constant companion. My counselor encouraged me to consider an anti-anxiety medication. Boy, that was hard for me!

I had been in twelve step recovery for years by this point, and there was a prevailing belief that any medication that helped manage feelings constituted a relapse.

When I resisted based on what I had been taught, my counselor explained that my amygdala had been in overdrive so long it might never calm down on its own. He explained that certain anti- anxiety medications can make a person feel high or drunk. However, others do not make a person high, they just help the amygdala synapses work better and calm down.

I was desperate to feel better, so I agreed to begin the non-mood-altering anti-anxiety medications. They help me to this day, and I am so grateful.

As I also struggled in counseling with the overwhelming guilt of not knowing my girls were being abused, it really helped me when the counselor told me, "Of course you didn't know. You don't think like someone with perverted intent toward a child."

Somehow that made sense to me and comforted me. Actually, it saved my life and my sanity.

I also worked with a second counselor during that season of life. She worked for the adoption agency, and our work focused on my feelings about giving my children up for adoption. She told me, "When someone can ask you if you have children and you say 'no,' without having to feel like you need to explain unless you want to that's when you will know you are healing." She was right.

64: Cancer, For Real

After my first bout in counseling, my life and my recovery rocked along for a while.

Then I began having abdominal pain. At the time, where I worked did not offer health insurance. Lack of insurance and the fact that I really don't like to go to the doctor meant that I did not seek care until the pain became unbearable.

The physician I eventually saw, an Indian woman, recommended a hysterectomy. When I woke up after

surgery she asked me, "Do you believe in God?"

I responded, "Yeah, I guess so."

She told me, "God must have been keeping you alive. You had uterine and ovarian cancer everywhere." I never had chemo. That was 1987.

Again, God has been so merciful to me.

65: He Picked Up a Woman

By this time, Don and I had been in a relationship for about five years. As I said before, we were crazy about each other, and he had tried to be really supportive.

It had, however, been a horrid season in our lives. I really had not been a fun person to be around for a long time. All the struggle and agony of surrendering the children, the gut- wrenching discovery of their abuse, and the protracted belly pain followed by surgery that left me with no hormones. I was coming even further apart.

Don reached the breaking point of his coping skills.

Though also in recovery from alcoholism, thankfully, Don didn't pick up a drink. He picked up a woman. Don had an affair with a fellow member of the Fifth Chapter.

Thankfully, I didn't pick up a drink either. However, back to therapy I went.

66: Spiritual Seeking & Aliases

I wish I could tell you I coped perfectly with all of that. I did not.

On some level, I was functioning better than I ever had in my life. But, I had a sense there was a hole in my soul. To fill it, I tried everything. I was an indiscriminate spiritual seeker: I went to a Unitarian church. I had tarot cards read. I went to a hooba booba palm reader. I thought I was going to literally melt in an Indian sweat lodge one time. I tried every Blessed Be Bologna Baptist church I could find.

Nothing filled the void.

Too, I started to date other guys. One guy I dated was a fellow named Jim who always carried a briefcase. I met him at meetings, and I initially thought he was very funny. Somehow it did not penetrate my consciousness that the fact he had no place to go, no job and no money should be warning signs.

Over time, he came to stay with me. Remember my mentality back then: As long as I have a guy, I am okay. Too, my middle name should have been F U N.

He had a lot of swagger and wanted to rush me into marrying him. Though I did not want to marry him, Jim did get me to accept a ring. I told him I wasn't accepting it as an engagement ring. In truth, I only accepted it because I liked the ring. Also, I didn't want to rush into marriage because I was messing around with Don on the side.

Even though Don was involved with the Fifth Chapter member who he had an affair with, he and I still hooked up occasionally. In my twisted way of thinking, I wasn't cheating with him because I was not in a relationship with anyone else. From today's vantage point, I am so sad that the woman I was then did not value herself any more than to settle for crumbs and toxicity.

As I got to know Jim more, I came to realize that not only was Jim humorously funny, he was weird funny. Actually, he was a nutter from the planet Crazy. With this growing awareness, I tried two times to break up with him. Both times, he talked me out of it.

Things came to a head one day when I was meeting with my girlfriends. They were all over me that he was strange and telling me to get him out of my life.

My desire to stick up for the underdog kicked in, and I started defending him.

However, I did comment, "He's not home right now, and he did leave that briefcase under the couch. We could open it up and see what's inside."

Like a bunch of middle-schoolers, we all went giggling to my house, got the case and opened it. Inside we found all these IDs with his picture but different names. Also there were a letter from someone outlining how he had ripped her off while he was using another identity.

All the sudden the blinders came off my eyes. Immediately, I was like, "Right! I gotta get rid of him! He's a pathological liar, and I can't count on anything he says."

At the time, I was living in a little apartment in Boca Raton inside a brick building. When he returned that night, I didn't even let him come inside. I handed him his briefcase and informed him, "We're through."

Though he tried, again, to talk me out of it, I was resolute. When Jim realized I was immovable in my decision, he punched the brick wall as hard as he could, literally blowing his fingers to smithereens.

Though I did take him to the hospital that night, once we arrived, I told the hospital staff, "I barely know the guy. I am not signing anything. I am not paying anything!"

As quickly as I could, I left the hospital not letting the door hit me where the good Lord split me!

That experience convinced me that my relationship skills were toxic, and I needed to get away from everything people, places and things.

67: Moving

I started thinking about moving away from Florida. I'm not a beach person, really. Though I like visiting the beach at night, I don't enjoy being on the beach during the day or swimming in the ocean.

My friends were *totally* against the idea. "You're leaving your support system, and you're going to get drunk," they said.

I was 38 at the time, and I had been working with the same computer firm for eleven years. At the same time, I knew I had to leave before I got too old and too scared to do anything.

So, I remained adamant and narrowed my choices to between Georgia and California. I had a bunch of friends from the Fifth Chapter in California. A woman I had sponsored, Nina, and her partner, Violet, lived in Atlanta.

I carefully reviewed the pros and cons of each location. The determining factors for me?

California had earthquakes, and I didn't like that. Though Georgia had hurricanes and tornadoes, I was used to that in Florida. Too, California was very expensive, and Georgia seemed much cheaper. Therefore, I decided to begin looking for work toward making a move to Georgia.

In retrospect, I can see how God was orchestrating my steps.

As soon as I decided on Georgia, Violet and Nina would send me the Atlanta Journal Constitution so that I could look for a job in the want ads.

I responded to an advertisement for a turn-around opportunity in a medical practice software company in Norcross. To interview I flew up on a weekend.

During the interview, they described the need to implement an incentive plan to stem the tide of employee turnover. I was confident I could do that, given my years of experience in the software industry.

On the spot, they offered me the job and agreed to pay for my move. I had enough time that weekend to accept the job, to rent an apartment and to fly back to be at work in Florida on Monday.

68: Dinner with My Brothers

As I was readying to leave Florida, though I had not interacted with them in the years since I placed the girls for adoption, I thought it would be good to meet my brothers for dinner as a sort of closure, I guess. Why we had not interacted, I am not really sure. I think I assumed that they sided with my parents and did not want anything to do with me. Anyway, we met for dinner.

I told them I wanted to say goodbye, that I had gotten a good job and was moving to Atlanta.

During the meal, Cal was talking about our upbringing like it was Ward and June Cleaver.

Finn and I were like, "What the hell is the matter with you? It was totally messed up."

Cal got really upset. He went into the restaurant's bathroom and would *not* come back out to the table.

Little did I know that it would be 23 years before we would speak again.

69: Georgia Jobs

When I was renting my apartment in Norcross, I thought it was close to the airport where the office was. Boy, was I wrong! So, I drove an hour a day each way from my apartment to the office.

Outwardly, I had it all: a new Camaro, a nice apartment, and power suits. The software I was representing was excellent. Inwardly, however, though counseling helped me get on much more stable terrain, I was still wracked with a significant degree of anxiety, not knowing where I fit in, and looking for someone to love me.

While I worked there, I loved the owner's wife, Charlene, so much. She was bubbly and a lot of fun, so we were a good match.

Though I loved working with Charlene and she really tried to make things better, I only worked for the medical office practice software for about eight months. The issue was her husband, Jack's, anger. I have not before or since known a person who would get so angry when he did not get his way that he would have nosebleeds.

My time with the company came to an end because, though he had cleared incentive plans for employees before I started implementing them, he decided he did not want to pay the earned bonuses.

I protested, "You can't do that!"

He responded, "If you don't do what I say, I'm going to fire you. I will give you 24 hours to decide."

Even in my active addiction, I had never been fired. Though I was not yet a Christian, I knew I had to look at myself in the mirror. So, I went in the next day and told him I would not tell the employees they were not getting their bonuses.

He said, "You're fired. I'll do it as layoff, but you have to sign something saying you're not going to come back and sue us."

Despite all that I had lived through, I thought that was the worst thing that could ever happen. My work ethic is so strong! Thankfully, by now, I had reached the point of determination about my recovery that no matter what using was not an option.

In very short order, I was hired by another medical software firm. Though the company was based out of Tucson, they were hiring in Georgia. I was hired to travel and teach doctors how to use what was then the new technology of allowing remote reading of X rays. In that position, I traveled all week, each week. I would fly out on Monday mornings and return on Fridays.

After I had been working there about six months, a new operations manager was hired. I heard from colleagues that he wanted all male staff.

One Monday, I had been out sick. The operations manager told me, "You've been out. We are downsizing, and I am going to have to let you go."

I was awarded unemployment. Though I had heard a rumor that there really was no downsizing rather, gender bias, I did not have the energy to pursue it.

70: Still Seeking

In short order, I lost my apartment because I had no income. Violet and Nina invited me to come and live with them. I gratefully agreed. Though I am clearly heterosexual and they are gay, my attitude was, "Anybody can do anything as long as they don't try to make me do it."

While I was living with them, I would visit the Little Five Points neighborhood on the weekend with friends from work. Despite all my wild living in my active addiction, I saw things there that I had never experienced!

For example, I saw a man leading a woman on a leash with a dog collar around her neck. I saw a woman walking in a leather vest and mini skirt whose back was nothing but strips so that her butt was fully exposed. I felt like Rebecca of Sunnybrook Farm, and my shocked reactions kept my friends rolling with laughter. In retrospect, God had protected me from so much during my drinking and using journey!

I remained leery on the whole God thing and a seeker all at the same time. I remember one visit when I went downtown to Peachtree Unitarian. I arrived just as church was just about to start. Once I was seated, I started realizing the church was filled with only openly gay couples except for me. Then, an obviously effeminate male began preaching.

Strangely, though I had many gay friends, I felt so uncomfortable. I did not want to make a spectacle of getting up, but as soon as church was over, I said, "Look at the time! I have a pressing engagement, and I must go!"

After that experience, I resolutely stated, "I am through with church!"

Living with Violet and Nina was good for a while, but they argued a lot and had much drama between them. In short order, I knew I needed to get away from their conflict as soon as I could, so I started to look for work and an apartment on the south side of Atlanta.

As a result of responding to a blind ad in the paper, I got a job as an administrative assistant to the general manager for a logistics firm near the airport.

I moved to a small town south of the airport to a duplex I loved. Also, my boss and I really liked each other; we were good friends. Though we slept together a couple of times, we decided we did not want to screw up our friendship - pun intended - and stopped.

71: A Different Kind of Church

As Scripture says, the Lord is not in the fire but in a still, small voice. (1 Kings 19: 11-13 NKJV).

While working at the logistics firm, I was having a lot of money problems and car troubles. One day when complaining about all that, I met a girl named Donna whose husband was a police officer.

Nearly every time she saw me at work there after she invited me to come with her to church. Honestly, she irritated me. However, she persisted. Eventually, she wore me down, and I agreed to go to church with them.

The first day, they invited me over for breakfast before we went to church. Their home church was like a rock 'n' roll church. People were dressed all sorts of ways from jeans to typical dressy church clothes. People looked glad to be there. I had never seen anything like that, and I thought it was weird as hell.

At the same time, I thought, "These people are nice. I could come here." After all, everybody wants to have a place where they belong, to have real friendships and real relationships.

My paranoia and defensiveness remained near the surface, however. I knew I did not want to be a notch in anyone's salvation belt.

After I had been attending for a few months, I went up to the pastor and said, "Look, I'm new here. I need you to know that I smoke. I have tattoos, and I'm not giving you any money."

He laughed and laughed at that. When he finally responded, he said, "Fair enough!"

The pastor was so smart in his response to me. If he had acted even remotely religious, I would have run. I had so much shame!

But God's purposes will not be swayed. It wouldn't be long before I came to Christ.

New Life Outside a Closed Chick-Fil-A

Shortly after challenging the pastor, I was sitting at a nearby mall. I remember sitting at a table outside the Chick fil A while it was closed. It was quiet, and I was alone. I had an overwhelming awareness that God had been chasing me. I put my head down on the table and quietly said, "I surrender. I give up. I give up. All I am, I surrender."

I had no glory hallelujah moment. I just thought, "It's done."

I had no real understanding of the ramifications of that surrender. Only later did I ask Him to forgive my sins. I did not understand, then, that with that decision He made me new, that He would heal me in places I didn't even know needed healing at the time.

Many Christians assert that the only way people can overcome alcohol and drug addiction is through Christ. This I know: If someone had tried to push Jesus on me when I was first trying to get sober, I would have died in addiction. My hurt and anger at God about not answering my prayers and saving me from the abuse as a child clogged out any incoming messages of faith.

Also, the overwhelming bitterness I felt toward my father and the guilt-intending, confusing messages of Catholic school warped my mind and heart for many, many years. For me, treatment and twelve step communities helped me stop drinking and using. They kept me alive until my mind and heart were clear enough to receive messages of grace and surrender to Christ.

73:
The Couples Class
& the Love of My Life

I told everybody I knew at church about my decision. Of course, they were happy for me. In short order, I got baptized. I started going to Sunday School in a couples' class.

In just a few weeks, people in the couples' class started bugging me to go to the singles' class. I did not want to go to a singles' class because I thought singles' classes were for the desperate losers who could not otherwise get a date. You see, after I came to Christ, my approach with men changed. I had a standard speech, "Look, if you want to go have fun without expectation of sex or marriage, I am your girl. Otherwise, I'm not."

Eventually, though, I did go to the singles class in June of that year. Surprisingly, the day of my first visit, I was actually a few minutes early. If you knew me, you would know that is a *big* deal. Though I am *always* on time for work, I am notoriously late everywhere else.

When I arrived at the room, there was only one other person there, William Deere. I thought he was *so* good looking. I lost the ability to speak. Because my favorite color is purple, one of the first things I noticed was his platinum ring with a square amethyst, which his brother had brought back from Vietnam.

In short order, he got my phone number. In July of that year, Will and I started dating.

As we started dating, I learned that Will, too, had an up and down past. However, he was a committed Christian. To me, that means he was doing Bible study, trying to order his life by God's word, and consistently attending church.

Like me, Will had been married before. He had a daughter, Erin, by that marriage. She was 5 years old at that time. She was beautiful, so precious! I also learned that, four years older than me, Will had a quadruple by pass surgery on his heart at age 34.

Amazingly, when that happened, he went to the hospital complaining with indigestion. They sent him home. When his blood work came back, they called him on the job saying, "Don't be alarmed, but come to the hospital now. Don't drive yourself." When he arrived at the hospital, he was immediately wheeled to heart surgery where the bypasses were performed.

Around Valentine's Day, we got engaged. At that time, we committed ourselves to sexual purity until we married.

In March, it was determined that Will had a serious and chronic heart condition. He must have a defibrillator and could not work anymore.

When we visited a lawyer about getting his disability started, the lawyer commented that it is rare that relationships remain committed once disability is discovered.

However, we loved each other, and I was committed to him. In June 1998, we married.

A Drinking Alcoholic
Will had been a social drinker while we were dating. After he could no longer work, he started drinking more. His drinking escalated to the point that, two months after our marriage, I had deteriorated to throwing soda in his face in frustration and had decided I was going to leave him. My decision was so well developed that I had arranged an alternate place to live.

Just as that occurred, out of the blue, a Bible study teacher from the church and his wife, Dan and Pat, called saying they wanted to have us over for dinner. We went, and they shared that they had a feeling we were in big trouble.

I thought, "Holy cow! This God thing must be really real."

Will admitted his drinking, and I confessed my plan to leave him. We finished the night on our knees praying and rededicating ourselves to Christ. Though things were not perfect from there by any means that was a major turning point in God making us new.

Character Transformation Begins Bit by Bit
Without a doubt, my involvement in twelve step recovery helped me stay sober and helped save my life. Twelve step groups are so focused on the problems of alcoholism and drug addiction.

I really needed that, especially during the first five years of my recovery when I was learning to be social without being drug affected. That said, my life and my character only started to transform after I came to Christ.

Why? Until I came to Christ, I didn't think much about right or wrong. There's not a lot about morals in twelve-step work. There was this whole aspect of my character that still needed to be developed.

Until I became a Christian, I didn't think twice about sleeping with guys, even married ones. Until Will and I learned to love one another with the love of Christ. I never dreamed I could be in a committed until death relationship. In my previous relationships, it was about, "What are you going to do for me?" With Will, I really cared about being a good and Godly wife.

When I became a Christian, I saw people whose lives were *different*. They were real, and in their lives I saw the love of Christ. I wanted what they had. So, just like I had in recovery, I hung around with them and did what they did.

I was blessed that Will wanted a real and deep relationship with Christ, too. So, Will and I hung out with people whose faith made a difference in their lives. We went all over listening to preaching. We read the Bible every day, and over time it transformed our minds and our desires.

Some of the stuff was harder for us to let go, like listening to Sneaker Pimps, AC/DC, Cracker – transitioning from head banger music to Christian music. For others, it might be something different, but for us it was music.

Over time, I surrendered more and more of my life to Christ and started focusing on developing my walk with God. I learned to look for the Holy Spirit's activity, to wait and see how Christ answers a situation. I learned to live a life of hope based my identity in Christ and based on God's promises for believers.

At the same time, I cannot stress enough that my growth as a Christian has been gradual. Though we rededicated ourselves to Christ that night, it took Will a while to accept his disability and inability to work. From the world's perspective, a man's identity is so tied up in his ability to work and provide!

As Will struggled, especially initially, he continued drinking. Resolute in protecting my sobriety, I would not even touch his drinks. During this same time, I had begun co-leading Christian twelve-step recovery groups through the church.

Can I tell you something that, to this day, grinds my gears? It makes my teeth itch how misogynistic some aspects of church culture can be! Though I had seventeen years' continuous sobriety, church leadership designated a man with less than a year's sobriety from crack cocaine as the group leader and me as the co-leader.

In short order, that fellow was doing crack again. I take comfort, however, in the fact that many people were helped through those groups.

Often, back then, when we were on our way home, Will would ask me to stop at the store so that he could buy beer. He would drink it in the car on the way home. Here I was staying sober and leading recovery groups yet going home with an alcoholic!

I hung in with my marriage, though, because I could see that Will and I were also doing the things that helped us grow in Jesus: personal Bible study, prayer, church attendance, a social circle of Christian friends, and seeking to order our day-to-day lives by God's word, bit by bit.

I am so grateful to say that, just as Jesus healed me bit by bit, He did that for Will, too. At the time of his death in October 2010, Will had 11 years of continuous sobriety.

Over the years, we hung with people committed to growing in their walks with God. There is truth to the saying, "Often faith is not taught, it's caught."

I wanted the depth and peace I saw in their lives, so I did what they did. This included regular church attendance, special trips to listen to Christian concerts or good preaching, a regular time of personal prayer and Bible study, and friendships with people committed to their walk with God.

Another aspect that helped me grow was reading books authored by those committed to their faith. Some of my favorite authors include Charles Colson, Max Lucado, Beth Moore, Joyce Meyer, Charles Swindoll, Warren Weirsbe and Phillip Yancey. Given my struggles with my thinking, Joyce Meyer's *Battlefield of the Mind* has been particularly helpful.

Smoking

Though I had achieved sobriety from alcohol and other mood-altering drugs, and though I was growing in my walk with God, I continued to smoke for years. I tried to quit smoking over and over and over again, but I just couldn't kick it.

I tried cold turkey. I tried with Wellbutrin. I prayed. I tried with the nicotine gum. The withdrawal was so intense, and it made my anxiety worse.

Over time, I developed pretty significant asthma and a wicked cough. One day, as I was having a coughing fit, generally chill Will *lost* it! He made it clear to me in no uncertain terms that he was worried about my health and that he feared losing me. Seeing the pain and worry in his eyes spurred me to a new level of action for no human had ever loved me like he did.

Using a nicotine patch, I *finally* was able to stop. Though I still use half a patch to this day, I have not had a cigarette in many, many years.

My message in sharing that with you? Again, I say, my recovery and growth in my spiritual walk has come inch by inch and bit by bit. Celebrate *every* success.

Will and I grew incredibly individually and as a couple during our marriage and we made many wonderful memories together. Over the years, we developed deep and enduring, precious friendships. I could not forecast how lifesaving those friendships would become.

The Long Valley of the Shadow

Life in recovery, or life as a Christian, is not always easy. At the same time that Will and I were building a happy marriage, we also dealt with periods of unemployment, lots of bills, and medical challenges with Will's heart condition.

Life is like that: parallel tracks of joys and challenges. Drinking or using might blot things out temporarily, but it only adds to your sorrow long term. Through I sometimes cried and worried, drinking or using was not an option for me when things were hard.

In October 2010, Will again entered the hospital. I thought of it as just another admission in the long succession of admissions. We had a wonderful time with friends while visiting him before I left to go home.

In the middle of the night, the phone rang. A nurse's voice matter-of-factly told me Will had died. As I exhaled my next breath, a keening sound I did not recognize as human escaped my lips. Somehow, I got myself together enough to call one of our close friends.

The next weeks and months were a blur of darkness. All I remember was sorrow and pain.

I moved numbly through the funeral planning, agreeing to whatever the planner said. I barely remember Will's funeral.

Grief like I had never known swallowed me. Devoted friends stayed with me, cooked for me. They loved me with their lives and their actions while I just focused on taking my next breath.

Taking a drink or a drug remained a non-option for me though, and I am grateful.

When his disability income stopped, my financial challenges multiplied. Hospital bills and an exorbitant bill from the funeral home added to the normal financial load. Our house went into foreclosure. The bill collectors started calling. I told them, "Look, my husband died. I have no money. Do what you gotta do. You can't hurt me any more than I'm already hurting."

I sold everything I owned except the essentials.

Friends even encouraged me to rehome our three Boston terriers to save money. I couldn't. Their unconditional love helped soothe me. I just focused on breathing and doing the next right thing through my fog of grief. Dear friends stayed close.

Because of his long-standing heart condition, Will had only a small life insurance policy. After the bank took our home, I bought a small cottage that needed a *lot* of work.

Friends from church pitched in and updated the electricity and the kitchen, repaired the bathroom and painted the house throughout. Yet again, God proved his faithfulness to me through the loving hands and muscles of His saints.

Misery Becomes Ministry Again
About a year and a half after Will died, God guided my path to cross with that of an old friend. We'd attended the same church years before and been casual friends, but she had moved to a different town. When we reconnected, I learned that her husband had recently had an affair and left their family. She was experiencing blinding grief like I had when Will died but for different reasons.

Just as it helps me remember how far I've come in recovery when I talk to a newcomer, it helped my lingering grief to help her, too. We listened to one another. We cried together about our losses until we laughed. Too, we laughed until we cried.

Over those months, God used even more of my past misery to minister to her, especially as she discovered her husband had been abusing her children.

I remember how my sanity was saved, all those years before, by the counselor telling me that of course I didn't know the abuse was happening because my mind doesn't think like an abuser. My reminding her of the same helped alleviate the unwarranted guilt that nearly crushed her. I'm so grateful that our misery can become our ministry!

Too, I'm so grateful that sharing the truth about our lives with ones who'll listen is what builds the most meaningful relationships. Today, she and I are heart sisters. She's the one who encouraged me that sharing my story might help someone else. She calls me a "true redemption story" and "a trophy of His grace."

Because of the trauma of my past, it can be hard for me to accept that encouragement. But, she persists!

In truth, I'm really glad.

Another way my misery has become my ministry is the work that have done for about the past ten years. In Georgia, there are certification programs for people in recovery from mental health challenges and or substance use disorders. Upon certification, there are numerous job opportunities to work with people seeking recovery. I am so grateful to be able to go to work every day where I can live my recovery out loud, and serve as a living example that *recovery is real and possible for anyone.*

Reconnecting with My Brothers

I know Will would want me to go on living well. I cherish having had his love for as long as I did.

One great blessing of my life since he died is that I have reconnected with my brothers.

In 2014, out of the blue, I got a Christmas present from my oldest brother. At first, it scared me. However, since then, we have had several nice visits.

Today, all of us acknowledge that growing up O'Brien was *crazy*.

They've each made their way in the world, married with good careers. Neither have children of their own.

Are my relationships with them all I hope for? No. My time in recovery and therapy has made me value relationships that have heart intimacy. They are not there yet.

However, there is peace in accepting things as they are. After all the grace I've been extended, how can I not extend grace that they are relating as best they can?

74:
Living a Life of Joy & Service in Challenge

Though life has become good again since Will died, there have been many struggles, too. Financial challenges, questions of God, and periods of great loneliness. There's a part of me that would love to find another mate, but dating again can be so challenging, as my few dates have proven! We'll just have to see how it goes.

Too, my body is showing signs of aging and the consequences of my past choices. My years of meth use have made my teeth porous. My having been a preemie on top of years of smoking have resulted in severe chronic obstructive pulmonary disease and oxygen dependence.

Also, in the fall of 2021, I was diagnosed with large cell lung cancer. Because of my COPD, immunotherapy not chemotherapy is my treatment option. COPD also makes the ability to receive radiation unlikely, for it is very hard for me to lie on my back as would be required.

Though those things are true, I press on. I purpose in my heart to live a life of joy and of service, to find the good in each day. I choose to realize that, even with the daily challenges, I am richly blessed.

75:

The Insidiousness of Addiction

Oh, how insidious is the nature of addiction. Sometimes the compulsion to use still returns to me, though I now have nearly 41 years of continuous sobriety. The urge to use returns most strongly at least for me near my sobriety anniversary, March 30.

I have learned to think, "Oh well, I'm getting homesick for the gutter. Using is not an option." Even today, I must do what I know helps me protect my sobriety cultivating honesty, accountability, gratitude and a spiritual practice. I keep my doctors informed about my use history. I stay away from playgrounds and mood-altering chemicals.

Protecting my sobriety is a priority in my life.

76: Choose Well.
You are Worth It

Remember, some thought I was too far gone more than forty years ago, but I chose differently. As long as there is life, there is hope. Choose well, dear reader. You are worth it.

A Letter of Love

Dear Reader,

Know that God, in His sovereignty, allowed the circumstances of my childhood of my life for my ultimate good, His glory and as a source of ministry.

He protected me through my abuse and addiction, my anxiety, my resulting choices and consequences, homelessness, estrangement, surrendering my children, cancer, affairs, unemployment, the loss of my husband and my home, and disability.

Life is not perfect and it has challenges. However, today my heart is pure. My life is honest, transformed, meaningful, and full of joy.

The hope of my heart is that - through my story individuals, families and churches will see the destructiveness of pretense and the healing, transformative power of transparency with each other and with Him.

I hope all will see that recovery is real and possible no matter the past. Thank you for joining me on the journey.

Know this: What has been possible for me is possible for you, too.

All my love,
Bea

Appendix 1:
Important Questions You Might Consider

Do you want recovery from an alcohol or other substance use disorder? Some other addiction?

Don't drink or use and get to a meeting. Don't give up. Do the work, and you can recover.

Do you love someone who struggles with alcohol or other drugs? Some other addiction?

Don't give up. God is working. Stay out of His way. Maintain an attitude of love toward that individual, but don't take any responsibility (money, work, chore, or obligation) that should naturally be theirs.

Do you want a relationship with Jesus?

Talk to God like you would talk to a friend:

God, I'm so sorry for the things I've done wrong, and I want to change. Thank you, Jesus, for dying on the cross as payment for my wrongs and rising from the grave to give me victory in this life and eternity. Come into my heart right now to live through the Holy Spirit. From now on, You are the boss of my life. Thank you. Amen.
Do you want to grow in your faith?

Find a church and a pastor that is authentic, where "words match feet." Look for a place that has a heart for people, teaches the Bible, and stresses a *relationship* with Jesus, not rules for right and wrong.

Go regularly. Find the people whose life is made different by their faith, and do what they do.

Appendix 2: Recovery Support Groups

Adult Children of Alcoholics
www.adultchildren.org

Alanon
www.alanon.org

Alcoholics Anonymous
www.aa.org

Celebrate Recovery
www.celebraterecovery.com/

Cocaine Anonymous
www.ca.org

Narcotics Anonymous
www.na.org

Recovery Dharma
https://recoverydharma.org/

Secular AA
https://secularaa.org/

Treatment Resources
https://findtreatment.samhsa.gov/

Reformers Unanimous
https://rurecovery.com

Appendix 3:
Simple Relaxation & Deep Breathing Practice

When we feel anxious or scared, we tend to breathe more shallowly and up high in our chests. Learning to practice diaphragmatic, or "belly," breathing can help us gear down.

1. Notice your body where you are standing, sitting or lying.
2. Notice where you are feeling tense.
3. Say in your mind, "I choose to begin to relax, letting the tension move out and away from my body." Adjust your body to be more comfortable, if you need to do so.
4. Close your mouth. You may also like to close your eyes.
5. Take a deep breath in through your nose like you are blowing a balloon up in your belly counting slowly "1 2 3" in your mind.
6. When you have taken in all the air you can, slowly release the breath through your mouth, counting a slow "1 2 3" in your mind.
7. Repeat five times, imagining your inhales and exhales as smooth, uninterrupted loops.
8. As you finish, lightly touch your thumb and forefinger together.

If you repeat these three times a day for seven days, you will notice your body beginning to "gear down" overall. With practice, the relaxed effect of this breathing can be triggered simply by touching your thumb and forefinger together.

Appendix 4:
Simple Mindfulness Practice
What is mindfulness?

In some twelve-step groups, you will hear, "Keep your mind where your behind is." That's a part of mindfulness practice. A more academic and inclusive definition is, "Paying attention to the present moment experience with open curiosity and a willingness to notice what is with without judgment."[1]

Another simple way to say it is learning to live fully in the here and now. Recovery Dharma identifies four foundations of mindfulness practice:
1. mindfulness of the body (breathing and bodily sensations),
2. mindfulness of feelings and feeling tones (pleasant, unpleasant or neutral),
3. mindfulness of the mind (either attachment or aversion), and
4. mindfulness of the mind or mental objects. Practicing the fourth foundation involves simply observing thoughts that arise as they float through and pass.

Recovery Dharma teaches that two practices help us develop mindfulness practice:

1. Inhale and exhale three deep, diaphragmatic breaths.
    a. Diaphragmatic breaths happen when you inhale like you are blowing up a balloon in your belly, even imagining inhaling air down into your pelvis, then exhale like you are helping your tummy to collapse. The first

breath, especially, focus on letting your shoulders relax downward.

2. Whenever negative or difficult self-talk arises in the mind, stop to ask yourself: a. Is it true?
   b. How am I sure?
   c. Am I certain that thoughts that seem automatic are true?
   d. How do I feel when I believe the thought?
   e. Who would I be if I didn't hold that belief?
   f. How would I feel if I held a different mindset?
   g. How would I feel if I held a different scenario in my mind?

[1]Adapted from Diana Winston, University of California, Los Angeles, Director of Mindfulness Education, Mindful Awareness Research Center

Cognitive Behavioral Therapy Worksheets
<u>Sample</u>

What is the activating event? *What has just happened that triggered the feelings I'm having?*
My boss walked by without speaking to me.

What is my initial belief about that event?
I think he doesn't like me. He's going to fire me!

What are my emotional consequences based on that initial belief? I feel frightened.

What evidence exists to dispute my initial belief?
I had a good performance appraisal, He spoke to me earlier in the day. He was walking quickly, looking intent on getting somewhere in a hurry.

What evidence exists to dispute my initial emotions?
I have always known him to be fair and consistent.

Template

What is the activating event?
What has just happened that triggered the feelings I'm having?

What is my initial belief about that event?

What are my emotional consequences based on that initial belief?

What evidence exists to dispute my initial belief?

What evidence exists to dispute my initial emotions?

Appendix 6: Scriptures that Helped Me Greatly

When I feel anxious ...

1 Peter 5:7	Casting all your care upon Him, for He cares for you.
2 Timothy 1:7	For God has not given us a spirit of fear, but of power and of love and of a sound mind.
Deuteronomy 3:22	You must not fear them, for the LORD Your God Himself fights for you.
Psalm 4:8	I will both lie down in peace, and sleep; For You alone, O LORD, make me dwell in safety.
Psalm 23:4	Yea, though I walk through the valley of the shadow of death, I will fear no evil; For You *are* with me; Your rod and Your staff, they comfort me.
Psalm 31:24	Be of good courage, And He shall strengthen your heart, All you who hope in the LORD.
Psalm 46: 1-3	God *is* our refuge and strength, A very present help in trouble. Therefore we will not fear, Even though the earth be removed, And though the mountains be carried into the midst of the sea; *Though* its waters roar *and* be troubled, *Though* the mountains shake with its swelling

When I feel discouraged ...

Psalm 42: 11   Why are you cast down, O my soul?
Hope in God, for yet again will I praise Him.

Reminders of His mercy and love ...

Psalm 41:10-13   But You, O LORD, be merciful to me,
and raise me up, That I may
repay them.
By this I know that
You are well pleased with me,
Because my enemy does not triumph
over me.
As for me, You uphold me in my
integrity,
And set me before Your face forever.
Blessed *be* the LORD God of Israel
From everlasting to everlasting!
Amen and Amen.

Psalm 94:18   If I say, "My foot slips,"
Your mercy, O LORD,
will hold me up.

Jeremiah 31:3   The LORD has appeared of old to me,
saying: "Yes, I have loved you with an
everlasting love; Therefore with loving
kindness I have drawn you."

Nahum 1:7	The LORD is good, a stronghold in the day of trouble; and He knoweth them that trust in Him.
Matthew 11:28	Come to Me, all *you* who labor and are heavy laden, and I will give you rest.
Romans 5:8	But God demonstrates His own love toward us, in that while we were still sinners, Christ died for us.
1 John 4:19	We love Him because He first loved us.

Reminders of how I am to live ...

Deuteronomy 13:4	You shall walk after the LORD your God and fear Him, and keep His commandments and obey His voice; you shall serve Him and hold fast to Him.
Psalm 91:1	He who dwells in the secret place of the Most High shall abide under the shadow of the Almighty

1 Peter 5:6-8	Therefore humble yourselves under the mighty hand of God, that He may exalt you in due time, casting all your care upon Him, for He cares for you.
James 1:2-4	Be sober, be vigilant; because your adversary the devil walks about like a roaring lion, seeking whom he may devour. My brethren, count it all joy when you fall into various trials, knowing that the testing of your faith produces patience. But let patience have *its* perfect work, that you may be perfect and complete, lacking nothing.
James 4:7	Therefore submit to God. Resist the devil and he will flee from you.

Reminders of how far I've come ...

2 Corinthians 5:17	Therefore, if anyone *is* in Christ, *he is* a new creation; old things have passed away; behold, all things have become new.
Psalm 30:11	You have turned for me my mourning into dancing; You have put off my sackcloth and clothed me with gladness.
Psalm 40:1-3	I waited patiently for the LORD, and He inclined his ear to me and heard my cry. He brought me up out of a horrible pit, Out of the miry clay, And set my feet upon a rock, *And* established my steps. He has put a new song in my mouth Praise to our God; Many will see *it* and fear, And will trust in the LORD.

Grace and peace to you from
God our Father and the Lord Jesus Christ.

Praise be to the God and Father of our Lord Jesus
Christ, who has blessed us in the heavenly realms
with every spiritual blessing in Christ.

For he chose us in him before the creation of the
world to be holy and blameless in his sight.

In love, he predestined us for adoption to sonship
through Jesus Christ, in accordance with his
pleasure and will— to the praise of his glorious
grace, which he has freely given us
in the One he loves.

In him we have redemption through his blood,
the forgiveness of sins, in accordance with the
riches of God's grace that he lavished on us.

With all wisdom and understanding, he made
known to us the mystery of his will
according to his good pleasure,
which he purposed in Christ,
to be put into effect
when the times reach their fulfillment—
to bring unity to all things in heaven and on earth
under Christ.

In him we were also chosen,
having been predestined according to the plan
of him who works out everything in conformity
with the purpose of his will, in order that we,
who were the first to put our hope in Christ,
might be for the praise of his glory.
And you also were included in Christ when you
heard the message of truth, the gospel of your
salvation.

When you believed,
you were marked in him with a seal,
the promised Holy Spirit,
who is a deposit guaranteeing our inheritance
until the redemption of those
who are God's possession—to the praise of his glory.
For this reason,
ever since I heard about your faith in the Lord
Jesus
and your love for all God's people,
I have not stopped giving thanks for you,
remembering you in my prayers.

I keep asking that the
God of our Lord Jesus Christ, the glorious Father,
may give you the Spirit of wisdom and revelation,
so that you may know him better.

I pray that the eyes of your heart
may be enlightened in order that you
may know the hope to which he has called you,
the riches of his glorious inheritance
in his holy people,
and his incomparably great power
for us who believe.
That power is the same
as the mighty strength he exerted when
he raised Christ from the dead
and seated him at his right hand
in the heavenly realms,
far above all rule and authority, power and dominion,
and every name that is invoked,
not only in the present age
but also in the one to come.
And God placed all things under his feet
and appointed him to be head over everything
for the church.
-- Ephesians 1:2-22 NIV

EPILOGUE

Beatrice Mary O'Brien Deere peacefully went to be with her Lord and Savior Jesus Christ at her home on March 12, 2022, surrounded by many who loved her. Born in Binghamton, New York, Bea had made Georgia her home for decades.

Bea was a trophy of restoration, redemption and grace. Her life was transformed, and she became transformative.

After surviving an incredibly traumatic childhood, Bea began her journey of recovery from anxiety and polysubstance use disorder March 30, 1981. One of the proudest achievements of her life: at the time of her death she had celebrated 40 years, 11 months and 10 days of continuous sobriety. During that time, she helped hundreds upon hundreds along their journeys of recovery. In fact, Bea worked as a certified mental health, addictive disease and whole health peer specialist as well as a certified psychosocial rehabilitation practitioner at McIntosh Trail Community Service Board and River Edge Behavioral Health for the last several years.

By Bea's own testimony, her life truly began to transform when she came to faith in Christ after eighteen years of sobriety and began to cultivate a daily relationship with Jesus. Soon after conversion, she met and married the love of her life, Will, and welcomed his daughter, Emily, into her heart. Will and Bea were joyously married and growing together in the Lord for 14 years until Will preceded Bea to heaven in 2010.

Since then, many from Bea's local faith and heart family wrapped her especially tightly, and Bea continued to serve faithfully at Mount Gilead Baptist as long as her health would allow.

It brought Bea great joy to reconciled with her brothers, Callahan and Finnegan and their spouses, in recent years.

Purity of heart and a loving orientation to others had so become Bea's moment-by-moment way of life. Evidence? She shared her faith with and ministered to her hospice nurse as one of the final conscious acts.

A service celebrating Bea's life will be held at 4:00 PM on Tuesday, March 15, 2022. Bea's beloved pastor, Fred Thompson, and her dear heart sister in Christ, Dr. Shannon Terrell Gordon, LCSW, CFRE, will officiate. Family and friends will visit for an hour after the service.

In lieu of flowers, please honor Bea's life with a gift to Mt. Gilead or River Edge Foundation to continue her legacy of restoration, redemption, grace and transformation. Bea's life will be further commemorated in a soon-to-be released book honoring her life and recovery title *You **Can Recover, Too!***

CELEBRATING BEA

Ms. Bea was my rainbow. When I think about a way to represent her, that's what I picture. Yes, she loved them, but she was so like one. There's the obvious reasons she was like one because she was so beautiful and colorful.

But, to me it was beyond the obvious because the purpose of a rainbow is to remind us of God's promise. That's what Ms. Bea did for me time and time again. She reminded me of God's promises. His love and faithfulness and mercy and grace and justice and might and power and care. The amount of times she prayed for me and encouraged me and pointed me to Jesus are too numerous to count. I didn't know how much I needed her until God gifted me with a relationship with her. And it's easily been one of the greatest gifts HE has ever given me.

I think one of the greatest testimonies of her life is everyone who was with her and who called her before she passed away knew exactly where she was going. There was no doubt in our minds she was going to Heaven to party with Jesus.

But I don't think it would honor Ms. Bea's memory completely to only talk about her serious side because, like a rainbow with its many colors, Ms. Bea had many sides. She made me laugh all the time. I loved that she could be so serious and so genuine and so funny all at the same time. She was larger than life, and she loved so well. There was not ever a time I left her house without feeling encouraged. There were several times I laughed so hard my stomach hurt when I was with her.

She was passionate and compassionate. She was loving and accepting. It didn't matter what you did or who you were, she loved and cared for all people she came into contact with. You could talk to her about literally anything from God and religion to jokes and games to hair and face masks. She was extremely transparent with everyone, and that is a quality I highly respected in her. She was a woman worthy to be imitated.

When I think about it, there's absolutely no way for me to ever put into words how amazing Ms. Bea was and the impact she had on my life. Even looking over this it's such a feeble attempt at it. There are no words to express everything she meant to me, everything she helped me through, everything she inspired me to do, and everything she made me want to be. I will forever be thankful for her life and grateful God let me be a part of it for a time.

Ehren Mercer

It is honestly very hard for me to come up here and talk for Bea. If anyone knows Mrs. Bea, they know that she always talked for herself. She always had an opinion, and they were always very good ones. She never let anyone walk all over her and she taught me to stay true to myself and to never allow anyone to hurt me.

While I was getting ready to leave for college, she sent me a message that said,

Stay focused, and work hard. Pray often, and stand up for what you know is right. Don't let others sway you, use you, or disrespect who you are. You're more than a conqueror not just because you are loved by so many people but because you are loved by the one true God. Stay real and stay in touch!

She made every feeling that I ever had and ever brought to her feel validated. She never let you leave without knowing that you were loved and cared for.

Mrs. Bea was a better friend to me than any friend I have ever had and, I believe, any friend I will ever have. I am heartbroken because I will never get to hold her hand again, cry with her, or hear her infectious laugh while I am on this earth. But, I am overjoyed that my sweet, God loving friend is with her Creator, breathing in the fresh air of heaven.

Julia Thompson

EULOGY

Do me a favor, please. Stand up and stretch right quick, will you?

Sharing what I need to you to know as one of my final gifts to Bea is going to take more than a minute or two. As my pastor says, "If you get done before I do, just slip out."

Too, because of how she grew up and all the work she did subsequently to develop a healthy life, the one thing that Bea could not abide more than anything was pretense and lack of authenticity. So, if you're not up for authenticity in these remarks, you might want to slip out also. This time is to honor my hero and my sweet bestie. Toward conveying the amazing miracle of her as a transformed trophy of His grace, I'm going to tell her truth as accurately as I know how.

Now, without the supernatural help of the Holy Spirit, I WILL NOT make it through this in a way you can understand. I have wailed and wailed and wailed in grief these last three days. If God doesn't do this, it won't get done. So, can we pray right quick?

Holy Spirit, I rely on You to speak words that honor Bea's triumphant and overcoming life. Hold back my tears sufficiently, God at least until the service is over - so that I can articulate clearly. Make me an instrument of your peace and comfort to those who loved her so at this time.

Oh God, if it would be Your will, use this time and continue to use her life to spread ripples of recovery, redemption and transformation from now until Jesus' return. We need you now. I trust you now. In Jesus' name, Amen.

We are here today to honor the life of Beatrice Mary O'Brien Deere. I am so incredibly honored that she asked that I do her eulogy. However, how can I possibly find the words to honor the life of someone whom God used to help save my life and my sanity during one of the darkest seasons of my life? And it was a LONG season.

I say, I say, I say her faithful, authentic friendship and hard won wisdom saved my life and my sanity when the world as I knew it literally blew apart, when I struggled to sift through the wreckage, when I was just trying to put one foot in front of the other to care for my children the best I could. Through that season, she became more than my best friend. She became my soul and spirit sister for more than the last decade.

How do you honor a life that is capable of that? I don't know, but in this holy time, I will give it my very best.

It happened like this.

I met Bea and Will when we were all in a Sunday School class at Mt. Gilead probably 2004 or so. I didn't know her well at all back then, but we were all faithful attenders. The things I remember from back then:

1. It was clear to me that Bea loved Jesus, was a student of His word. She was particularly drawn to the meanings of the names of God. Her love for his Word and her knowledge about the meaning of His names impressed me and drew me to her.

2. Once, we went to Will and Bea's house on Patton Road to a Sunday School party. Their pups Luna, DJ and O'Reilley were much younger dogs then. The dogs were SO energetic jumping up on me and all over the place, yapping. Her attempts to get them under control only revved them up. I suppose she picked up on my discomfort. In response, Bea got anxious and really talkative, as she did when anxiety was in her driver's seat. So three dogs are yapping and jumping. Bea is yelling at the dogs and talking 90 to nothing. I'm thinking, "Dear God, let me out of this house!", so I tried move quickly through the house to the back yard where their pool was. I stepped out onto the back deck to discover that Bea had been and continued to after she came outside (still talking!) putting dish detergent on the pool slide to try to help make it slippery so it would be more fun for everyone. As a result, there were bubbles EVERYWHERE.

3. I was WAAAAYYYY more uptight and inflexible in 2004 than I am today.

4. So, here I am, Ms. Uptight who has just made it through Jumping Yapland trying to get to 'safety' and landing in Bubble land. I turn around and I'm looking into Bea's big blue eyes right behind me her highly Clairol influenced blonde hair all askew from the pool and dealing with the dogs.

5. I am so ashamed to admit it today but I remember thinking, "I have landed in the Twilight zone. If I ever get out of here, I am NEVER coming back to this house."

6. We made it out onto the patio, and sat down. Bea lit a cigarette still just a talking! Me, Miss Religious back then, thought, "Smoking at a Sunday school party, the very idea!"

   Oh, how MUCH God has used to change me since then! Today, I'd say, "I'm so glad we are here together. Can I empty your ashtray?"

7. Back then, I remember thinking that she and I could never be close friends, we were far too dissimilar.

8. **Lesson 1 from her life: which I came to understand from her years later: Take time to understand the WHY of people's lives.** Why were her dogs so important to her? Why was it hard for her to discipline them? Why did she get so anxious when folks got uncomfortable around her? What was her intention with the dish detergent? What had her life been like before that day? What had she overcome to function as well as she did that day? Even taking time to consider those questions would have made even my internal thoughts **so** much different! I am eternally grateful to her for her patience and kindness teaching me that. People like me back then hurt her SO many times. Today, it breaks my heart to think that I used to be one of them not just to her but to many others.

9. **Lesson 2 from her life (which I learned from her in spades again, years later): When we take time to understand people's stories, we are far less likely to judge and much more likely to offer compassion.**

10. **Lesson 3 from her life which I learned from her and through God's allowing the circumstances of my life to beat me to a bloody pulp, leaving me desperate for nothing but grace and love.** My sole responsibility is to let God's love and grace flow through me to stay out of God's way when working in someone's life, NOT to judge or try to be their Holy Spirit.

    As Bea would say, "God told us to be fishers of men, not fish cleaners. It's our responsibility to catch them, His responsibility to clean them." Amen and amen, my sweet bestie. If you taught me anything, you taught me that people just want to be loved.

11. Anyway, Bea and I continued to see each other at church and were not much more than superficial friends.

12. Over time, our family changed churches then moved out of town, and Bea and I lost touch for several years.

13. I did not learn until 2011 that Will had died in October 2010. Even though we had been superficial friends, I KNEW how devoted they were to one another, so I reached out to her to express condolences. The rest, as they say, is history. **Isn't it so cool how, when we reach out to minister, so often, we are the ones who are the most blessed?**

When Bea and I came back together, I learned that, when Harvey Wilson took Will to the VA for what turned out to be his last visit, Will leaned against the wall trying to breathe and told Harvey, "Take care of Bea." And you have.

Kim, I am so sorry that sweet you had to be the one to have the last Saturday morning that you did, but you helped honor Will's last wish for his girl. Thank you.

May our Lord richly bless you both for your faithfulness to both of them.

When Bea and I came back together, I learned how **Jimmy and Joyce** Cochran, in their gentle way, had helped her find a home within her means when her house was foreclosed upon after Will died.

You have been such incredibly faithful friends to her, including her in family holiday gatherings, taking her to the doctor, so much more that only she and Jesus know. Know that she respected both of your gentle, faithful walks with Jesus so much. I grieve for you - and your family in your loss of her, given your loss of your precious daughter, Patti, this past September. Loss upon loss! May the Lord heal your hurting hearts?

Also, Joyce: your making chocolate covered cherry mice for Bea's birthday party after she'd been freaked out by having a rat in her house goes down in the history books as priceless, by the way.

When Bea and I came back together, I learned how **Debra and Jerry** Laabs continued Will's friendship with Jerry by wrapping around Will's girl. Thank you. You, too, Deb, were precious to her, have been so faithful to her…. Such a gentle, faithful servant of Jesus. As I've told you many times, I hurt with you in your loss of her, given your loss of your precious partner, Jerry, in January 2021. So much loss! You know how much I love your residual Texas drawl. We need a bawl date soon.

When Bea and I came back together, I learned how **the Mercers and the "Mercer kids"** as she called you until she died came together with others to help get her house on Poplar Street ready…. Serving with sweat, a testimony to your raisin' and your individual relationships with Jesus. Oh, how she has loved your visits, playing games with you, doing life with you over the years. Oh. How. She. Loved. You.

Denise, she so loved your deep talks about the Lord, valued your friendship so.. Just as she wouldn't even let me come around when I had walking pneumonia for weeks recently, she UNDERSTOOD that caring for your mom, COVID and injury consumed you recently. That didn't diminish your friendship.

Ehren, thank you, beyond words for calling me as I had done a boomerang back to Georgia from a business trip to get to her when she headed toward heaven so quickly on Saturday.

I will ALWAYS be grateful to you for giving me opportunity to say final good byes at least by phone to the lady who had become my hero, my soul sister. So grateful.

You are so right sweet young lady that Bea was a rainbow, reminding us all of God's promises AND bringing color and joy and fun to our lives. I, like you, cried til I laughed and laughed til I cried with her, so many times. Oh, how she loved you and loves you still.

People of Mount Gilead: Your behavior toward Bea has so encouraged me in the Lord. Like antibodies to a wound to heal it, you wrapped around her in love and inclusion, especially after Will died living out your faith and obedience to Scripture's admonitions to care for widows.

It has been beautiful to see the body of Christ being the Body to her. Every youth group trimming of her yard, every visit, every trip taking her to treatment.... You represented Jesus well. She so loved the teens Sunday school class she taught with Sam.

Fred and Mary: she loved you.... Loved your children too...

Then, there were **Ed and Doreen Palmer. And me. We** were her friends who had 'an edge' to us. When I met Doreen for the first time, I thought, "Thank God! Debra and Joyce are just so well SWEET. Doreen's a direct 'handle it' girl. I aspire to be as sweet as Joyce and Debra, but I'm .... not.

Ed and Doreen both loved Will and Bea for so many years! Please pray for Doreen, especially, for she couldn't be with us today. She surrendered her Ed to heaven at the end of February after more than 50 years of marriage. This live memorial service is just too much for her just yet, but she's watching online. Bea loved you, Doreen, as a precious sister in the Lord. She understands. Be still and know.

Judy Young, you were her heart partner at River Edge. She loved you, prayed for you, wanted you to take care of you. And then there was **me.**

I intended to reach out to Bea in ministry. Only God knew, at the time, that He'd use her to save my life and my sanity. She'd become the heart sister I got to choose.

About the time Bea and I reconnected, my former husband of 26 years deacon, Sunday school teacher, choir member who I thought adored us all abruptly left our family. I soon discovered that this same man that I and all adults who knew us had so respected had a very dark side in deep secret toward our three children for many years. My own precious children had been hurt under my nose and I did. not. know.

I was absolutely shattered with loss, overwhelmed with guilt, confused beyond description. My heart was so broken I had chest pain. It hurt to breathe, and I had 3 children 12, 14 and 19 at the time to provide for and parent

I tried to carry on with all that was in me and felt like I sucked at it at every turn. I tried to lean into my faith, to trust God. The only prayers I could muster were "Oh God…." "God you know…." I felt like I was drowning.

Many of my long-time friends never called, never came… acted awkward when they saw me… they didn't know what to do, I suppose…. and all they knew was that I was going through a divorce. But then, there was Bea.

Those of you who know her well know that she HATED to talk on the phone, preferred texting. But that sweet girl CALLED ME NEARLY EVERY DAY FOR ABOUT A YEAR. She listened. And she listened some more. She visited. And she listened. And she listened as I tried to make sense of what will never make any sense at all. Sometimes, she was tender and kind. Sometimes she was so blunt it HURT. Through it all, though, she STAYED. She shared the wisdom she'd worked HARD to mine from her own experiences to <u>save</u>. <u>my</u>. <u>life</u>.

And she sent at least 10,000 encouraging memes. Nobody ever got just one meme from Bea, right?

Who was with me when my former husband came to get his things from our home? Bea. How could I ever repay just THAT?

From her that day I learned the power of the questions, "What do you need from me right now? How can I help you best right now?" Another powerful lesson….

Sometimes, when we are with someone who is in SO much pain, they genuinely don't know how we can help. I learned from her that we can just STAY. Be lovingly and patiently present.

What a pair we have been through these years. On the surface, as different as night and day. She was short and blonde. I am tall and dark. I'm structured and traditional and tailored. She loved purple and sparkles and rainbows and butterflies and chatchskes.

She could have squirrel moments by the dozen, and I'm a planner supreme. My children call me vanilla. Bea died with a more than a little hippie in her soul. I'm typically large and in charge and fearless. **Though she had done so much work and come SO far to loosen anxiety's grip on her life, fear was a persistently besetting foe she'd wrestle to the ground repeatedly. Over and over, I saw her, "Do it afraid." Over and over I saw her feel the fear as an initial response and replace those thoughts with truth. And, sometimes fear won a round... temporarily.**

Anyway, God used her to help pull me through that D.... A.... R.... K season because she, too, had had experiences of an abuser showing one face in public and another at home. Her father. She, too, had had someone she trusted violate precious children without her knowledge. Her first husband.

Her therapist helped her not feel so guilty by saying, "Of course you didn't see it. You don't think like a person with harmful intention toward children." Just as Scripture teaches, she comforted wherewith she'd been comforted. She helped convince me I wasn't crazy and that I wasn't the worst mother who ever lived.

She loved and travailed in prayer over my children as they, too, were devastated and coped as best they knew how.... and that was a wild ride indeed. Lord have mercy, what a story we all have together! I am watching prayer after prayer of hers come true in their lives.

To give you a grin: part of our story included Bea really wanting to wear pierced earrings again after her earlobes split. She actually convinced me to try to glue them back together with Super Glue at our dining room table. Yep. We really did that. And I have a doctorate, for heavens' sake! Let me save you some trouble: You don't need to try it. It doesn't work!

Over time as Bea's and my relationship deepened, I learned more and more of her story. As we talked, she decided she wanted her story and the tools that helped her recover preserved in book form. **After all, her life became about others, didn't it?** Therefore, I had the privilege of recorded interviews with her for HOURS.

You know she could be both stubborn as a mule on steroids when she wanted to be and plagued with selfdoubt... sometimes within a span of 5 minutes.

Therefore, as was Bea's way, after she approved the copy, the book came back from the editor and we were selecting cover designs, she began to doubt that she had anything to say, that anyone would be interested, that it would be helpful. Though I tried to reassure her, she wanted to let it go to print "later" .... She approached it like she did her will, her power of attorney, etc..... Bless her soul.

Together- we translated them into a book. Every word is true.... Only the names have been changed to protect the innocent.... and the not so innocent, Bea among them at one time:).

Just last Thursday night, she told my now-husband, Scott, that she worried that her life didn't count for anything. Seriously?

If she'd not been so sick, I'd have spanked her. Joyce and Debra are too sweet to have done it, but I'd'a spanked her!

To reassure her, my sweet Scott thanked her for taking care of his girl before I was his girl, for looking after his kids before they were his kids, for accepting and loving him so quickly.

Her life DID count, if only for MY family.... and I KNOW we're not the only ones.

There are many in this room with similar stories, I know.... not to mention the HUNDREDS she helped along the journey of recovery during her nearly 41 years of continuous sobriety running Celebrate Recovery groups, working as a certified peer specialist, and people she met in the highways and byways of life. Oh yes, her life DID count indeed!

The book will soon be published as a memorial to her amazing life.

PLEASE join me in praying that her story will be heard round the world and bring the hope and healing that it has brought to those of us who had the privilege of meeting her this side of heaven, will you?

So what was her story? I'm so glad you asked! The very abridged version is this:

Beatrice Mary O'Brien Deere was born November 3, 1957 weighing only 1 pound 13 ounces. Her incubator was an iron lung; from her time in it she developed the slight rocking she continued throughout her life whenever she sat.

Bea's granddad O'Brien immigrated from Ireland, and her granddad scrapped to build a life of wealth and privilege for his family. Their son, Tom, was Bea's dad.

Bea was the middle child and only girl in her very New York Irish Catholic family. By Bea's report, her mom whom she favored tremendously/, by the way was the quintessential stay-at- home 50s housewife. Her dad, injured in Korean combat, came home with a serious back injury, a host of mental and emotional demons and a serious drinking problem. However, to the public, he was a pillar of the community and an entertainer supreme.

From the book:
People saw our wealth and thought we were the perfect family. We were members of the country club. Our family walked in the Thanksgiving Day parade. We vacationed in Miami Beach. Publicly, my parents were cultured.

It was all about appearances. Then, there was our life at home.

For a long time, my dad was (a).... functional alcoholic. But when he started drinking, it wasn't a question of if things would turn dark, it was a question of when.

From another book section:
The words he said to me were the worst: "I wish you'd never been born." "You are a troublemaker." "You are more trouble than you are worth." "You are stupid." "You are a loser."

What would make him stop? Nobody knew.
Nobody got help back then.

Bea endured her first bad beating from her father while in kindergarten, her legs and but too tender to touch for days. That precious, tiny, blonde child.

Verbal and physical violence occurred at least weekly, often daily, and often erupting unprovoked or when the children did something that had been previously okay.

Her little developing brain learned to live on high alert to survive. Therefore,

- Is it any wonder anxiety rooted itself within her?
- Is it any wonder then that, when I met her on the Yapland pool day, when she sensed my unease, anxiety was her first response?
- Is it any wonder she had to work to overcome self doubt?

Again, when we take the time to learn each other's' stories, compassion and patience is our more likely response.

At 5 or 6, her dad started giving her sips of his drinks to calm her. Also as recorded in the book,

By the time I was eight, I started praying every night that my parents would divorce or my dad would die. I wanted a way out of our life at home so badly! I started to think, "What kind of God is this? He's not helping us!"

Then, during the day, I was in Catholic school where the nuns reinforced talked about our going to hell and doing penance.

I wanted to believe in God so badly, but my concept of Him was terrible.

By second grade, she had a mouth at school. Bea with a mouth? Imagine that!

By age 9 she was stealing drinks.

She was sexually molested by a neighbor and ran away for the first time at 10 only to be brought home and told to be grateful for how good she had it. She couldn't go to the police because her dad's brother was policeman who guarded the mayor, and his other brother was a judge.

She waited. She endured. The hurt and frustration built like gunpowder in a bomb.

Trying to control her, her parents made her go to all girl's Catholic high school. She made good grades AND hung out with the boys, smoking and doing drugs. She held the record for the most suspensions from high school. Her dad bought her staying there with donations.

By the time she enrolled in college, she was drinking and using drugs to avoid withdrawal fully convinced that her drinking was the only thing (her words, not mine) "keeping her from the nuthouse."

Until she dropped out of college soon after surviving a gang rape, she maintained a 3.0 GPA though she rarely went to class or studied. If that's not evidence of her amazing intelligence, I don't know what is!

After she left college, today's time will only permit me to tell you that God continued to protect her and others from her active addiction over and over and over again.

When she was 23, Bea's drug dealer boyfriend bet her $1,000 she couldn't quit drinking. So, on March 30, 1981, Bea stopped drinking.

But there was a problem: her untreated withdrawal triggered cardiac arrest. She was revived by EMTs after they pulled unconscious from the complex's pool.

Neighbors she then considered "Holy Rollers" (Isn't that funny, given her ensuing devotion to Christ?) took her to detox.

In the early 80s, her treatment accommodations were a cot and a spoon wrapped in towel to protect her tongue if she began to sieze. She stayed because the cardiac arrest scared her and – she overheard the treatment team saying her prognosis for recovery was poor. That got her Irish up!

God uses the most unlikely things for good, doesn't He?

What transformed Bea Deere from the traumatized, terrified, active alcohol and drug addict to the wise, funny, loving soul in whom there was no guile that we knew and loved? I'm so glad you asked.

While she was in treatment, she was required to go to 3 AA meetings every day. When she started in AA and people would start to talk about a Higher Power, the wounded little girl inside who felt like God never heard her would emerge. She'd stand and shake her fist and say, "God? Harrumph! You people are weak! No GOD hears you! I know, because I prayed, and He didn't hear me."

People in the group would patiently say to her only, "Don't drink or use any drugs, and keep coming back." And she did.

There's another saying in recovery meetings, "It works if you work it." And she did. This is her AA Big Book. Do you see all the highlights? How worn it is from use?

She read it. She used it. She tried to learn it. She found the winners in the groups and stuck with them, did what they did.

Over time, she became open to the level of spirituality talked about in AA. Her first prayer?

"Dear God, please help me not hate that son of bitch so much!"

Aren't you so glad that our God is big enough for us to doubt that He is, to doubt that He hears, to grow impatient when He answers "slowly" because of His bigger redemptive purpose, to shake our fist, to swear when we start toward Him? I know I am!

Anyway, 18 years of faithfulness in the 12-step program continued. Bea changed bit by bit. From her own words from the interviews,

Over time, the hope that a good life could be mine began to take hold in my bruised heart. I shifted from having to stay clean to keep from dying to wanting to stay clean to have a better life. Those were the beginnings of my made-up mind that, "No matter what happens, I am not going to pick up a drink or a drug to cope with life!" When I started to have hope for myself, my motivation for recovery shifted from the shaky foundation of fear to the bedrock of determination to protect my recovery as a foundational building block of my life. Again, inch by inch and bit by bit.

Hear me clearly, her life in life in recovery was NOT easy. Multiple rocky and toxic relationships with men. Eviction. Working two jobs and ends still not meeting. Tremendous losses. Suicidal thoughts after betrayal discovered. Permanently disowned by her parents to the extent that she was not informed when her mother died and her father's obituary and will did not list her as his child. Now THAT gets my Irish up and I'm not even Irish!

23 years of estrangement from her siblings and other extended family. Yet she still didn't drink or use and kept going to meetings.

Through it all, in her words, "I remained leery on the whole God thing and a seeker all at the same time."

Just over 30 years ago, a co worker persisted in inviting her to her church so much that she irritated Bea, actually. In response to her gentle persistence, however, Bea went. Bea's words when I interviewed her in 2020?

"People were dressed all sorts of ways suits, jeans, anything...looked glad to be there... I thought it was weird as hell."

But she kept going. Her approach to the pastor after attending for a few months?

"Look, you need to know I smoke. I have tattoos, and I'm not giving you any money!" He laughed and told her that was fine, so she stayed.

Shortly after, sitting outside a closed Chick Fil A in a mall, in Bea's words:

I had an overwhelming awareness that God had been chasing me. I put my head down on the table and quietly said, "I surrender. I give up. I give up. All I am, I surrender."

I had no glory hallelujah moment. I just thought, "It's done."

I had no real understanding of the ramifications of that surrender. Only later did I ask Him to forgive my sins. I did not understand, then, that with that decision He made me new, that He would heal me in places I didn't even know needed healing at the time.

So how did God heal her after salvation? I'm so glad you asked.

Hear me, her life even with Jesus was anything but easy. Even before she and Will married, Will was declared disabled due to his heart condition. There were periods of her unemployment. Financial struggle. Will died. Her home was foreclosed. Periods of great loneliness for her mate. COPD. Lung cancer. How did she persist? Become better not bitter?

Can you see this Bible? Do you see these devotionals? See how they are written all over, pages dog-eared, worn?

God transformed her because, again, she hung with the winners people whose lives had been truly transformed by God and did what they did.

Day after day, year after year…. She got into the Word, and the Word got into her. The spirit of God used the Word of God and the people whose lives were transformed by God to walk with her into an ever-deepening walk with God.

Oh, how she loved the New King James Translation. Selections from her very favorite passage.... Psalm 27:

The LORD is my light and my salvation;
Whom shall I fear?
The LORD is the strength of my life;
Of whom shall I be afraid?
Though an army may encamp against me, My heart shall not fear; Though war may rise against me, In this I will be confident. For in the time of trouble He shall hide me.... He shall set me high upon a rock. **When my father and my mother forsake me, Then the LORD will take care of me.** ⋯⋯***I would have lost heart, unless I had believed That I would see the goodness of the LORD In the land of the living.*** *Wait on the LORD; Be of good courage, And He shall strengthen y our heart; Wait, I say, on the LORD!*

Given her life, is it any wonder that this was her favorite passage of all?

Her second favorite, Psalm 51. Let me share parts....

Have mercy upon me, O God, According to Your lovingkindness; According to the multitude of Your tender mercies. Wash me thoroughly from my iniquity, And cleanse me from my sin. Behold, You desire truth in the inward parts, And in the hidden part You will make me to know wisdom......

Create in me a clean heart, O God, And renew a steadfast spirit within me. And uphold me by Your generous Spirit.

Then I will teach transgressors Your ways, And sinners shall be converted to You. For You do not desire sacrifice, or else I would give it; You do not delight in burnt offering. ¹⁷ The sacrifices of God are a broken spirit, A broken and a contrite heart These, O God, You will not despise.

And she CLUNG to parts of Isaiah 43:
But now, thus says the LORD, who created you, "Fear not, for I have redeemed you; I have called you by your name; You are Mine.
When you pass through the waters, I will be with you; And through the rivers, they shall not overflow you.
When you walk through the fire, you shall not be burned, Nor shall the flame scorch you. For I am the LORD your God, The Holy One of Israel, your Savior; Since you were precious in My sight, And I have loved you; Fear not, for I am with you; ¹¹I, even I, am the LORD, And besides Me there is no savior.
¹....¹⁸ "Do not remember the former things, Nor consider the things of old. Behold, I will do a new thing, Now it shall spring forth; Shall you not know it? I will even make a road in the wilderness And rivers in the desert

When she called me last Tuesday to tell me the doctor had shortened her prognosis from 3 years to a year, the first concern she said to me? "I want to bring honor and glory to God."

When, Wednesday, the radiation oncologist couldn't help her and shortened her lifespan to three months, she told me, "I want to die well." Oh, my sweet bestie, you did. You did.

When she told me, Thursday, she wanted me to do her eulogy, I told her I'd have to be sure to include a blonde joke (for she LOVED them).

Though she was laboring to breathe, she slowly looked up and said with a straight face, "Why couldn't the blonde call 911?"

Joyce, Jimmy, Deb and I asked, "Why?"

Without missing a beat, she said, "Because she couldn't find 11 on the dial."

Bea to the very end!

Her horrific childhood. Treatment and AA's saving her life until the little girl so disappointed with God could heal enough to open her heart to Christ. The total transformation of her morals and character that began with her surrender to Christ making her a new creation and bloomed through her day by day growth in Him through the ensuing years.

She cooperated with God for Him to redeem it ALL, making her life MORE impactful because of it all. Our God is like that isn't He?

This eulogy is one of my final gifts to Bea, the sister I got to choose. I won't feel like I've honored what she would have wanted if I ended this without saying these things to all within the sound of my voice.

Here her raspy voice instead of mine, won't you?

- Do you struggle with anxiety? With past trauma? Reach out for help. It's available, you can heal. I did.
- Do drugs or alcohol have too big a hold on your life? Find a meeting. Treatment can help. You can be free. I was.
- Are you disappointed or hurt with God? That's okay. The God who preserved my life and transformed me bit by bit is big enough to handle it. Be honest about it. Stay open to the possibility that there's a bigger story than the hurt you feel today.
- Have you ever surrendered to Jesus? AA will help you stay sober, yes. Jesus will *change you,* transform you to be the very best version of yourself, who He created you to be… redeem your misery to ministry, your mess to a powerful message. He's right here. Right now. Waiting for you. Longing for you, actually. To make you knew. To heal you in places you don't even know need healing. Talk to Him now.

Bea's favorite hymn was Great is Thy Faithfulness as we sang earlier. As I was preparing these remarks, I was struck by how perfect the bridge from a more current remix is to describe God and Bea's life.

Beginning to end, my life's in Your hands.
Great, great is Thy faithfulness.
You never let go.
This one thing I know.
Great, great is Thy faithfulness.

Beatrice Mary O'Brien Deere, a trophy of God's grace and transformation. I love you, my sweet bestie. Thank you for being my hero.

Pour a little lemon juice in your caffeine free Diet Coke and tell blonde jokes to Jesus and Will til I get there, okay?

Thank y'all for listeniin'.

Dr. Shannon Terrell Gordon

Well, you've heard from Bea's closest friends. There should be no doubt in your minds that Bea was loved. Now you get to hear from her Pastor.

It's difficult to separate this part of my introduction to only Bea because Bea and her husband Will were already members of Mt Gilead when I got here. They were an unusual and unique couple. Both had pasts that included a lifestyle that was far removed from a Godly lifestyle, but God had transformed them both.

Both had a keen sense of humor and did not hesitate to be more than just members of the church but to also be friends of our family. They constantly invited us and especially our two girls to their home to go swimming.

When Will passed away it was a devastating blow to Bea because of their love for one another, and my family grieved with her.

Bea was no stranger to hardship. Without Will's income, she found herself searching for a home. Amazingly, God provided.

Bea remained faithful to the church-even singing in the choir. Just a few years ago she even began co teaching one of our youth's Sunday School classes. All this in spite of the fact that she was developing severe COPD and was dependent upon the oxygen bottles she was never without.

Her life was a constant growth and transformation by God's grace. I hadn't been here long when we had either a sharing time or in one of our church conferences in which Bea shared. I'll never forget the moment a not so "Sunday School" word slipped from her lips. Now, just to be certain you understand, it wasn't a majorly bad word but it was not one you'd use in church. Don't take this the wrong way.

I think if Bea were sitting here today, she'd laugh at what I'm about to say. We both would laugh and her laugh was contagious.

As her Pastor, sometimes Bea could be well, frustrating. If she had an idea or if she had a Scripture she didn't understand, she could be like a bulldog with a bone. She rarely asked me questions which had a simple answer. Often, they were questions that there will be no answer to this side of heaven.

Sometimes we'd be trying to begin a service or a Bible study and you'd hear one loud voice that continued talking yep, you got it, it was Bea. Or laughing it was a loud and contagious laugh.

Bea loved to laugh. She would email me cartoons that made her laugh, and she wanted to share the humor.

Once, when we were sharing testimonies, Bea let said a not so Sunday School word not often said in church. I don't think anyone even blinked an eye. They knew Bea's spiritual journey. By the way, I never heard her say that word again and I won't repeat it so don't ask.

I hesitate even saying this next thing but when I was born, my parents named me Fred and that's what I've always answered to most of my life just plain Fred. I've never been big on titles but once I became a Pastor, most people have insisted on referring to me as reverend (not fond of that one), preacher (okay), pastor, or Pastor Fred. But not Bea. She might use one of those titles but right now I think I can hear her laughing and calling me "Fast Freddy."

I told you not to take that the wrong way because I loved Bea because she was always honest and always herself. Bea was always Bea.

I loved her because she loved her church and always spoke positively of it.

I loved her because of the way she loved my family. She came alongside my family in some difficult times. She was an encourager.

It was her gift! She wanted to help people. She especially wanted to help those who had gotten caught in lifestyles far removed from a Godly lifestyle. She wanted them to find the freedom she had found in Jesus Christ.

And that leads me to what I loved most about her she was the poster child of a person who had been mightily transformed by the grace of God. That's why even when she did something frustrating, I usually found myself smiling. I don't know that she ever shared her whole testimony with me but there was a time when Bea came face to face with the fact that she was a lost sinner far removed from God.

She surrendered her heart, her mind, and her life to Jesus Christ as her Lord and Savior. I don't think she ever looked back. She loved Jesus and because of that she continued to grow in her faith. That's why she asked me some of those difficult questions she was growing.

I picture Bea in that story when Jesus was reclining at the table and the woman came and began crying and washing His feet with her tears and anointing Him with perfume. The host, Simon, was critical of Jesus because He allowed this sinful woman to touch Him. Jesus confronted Simon with a parable. It's found in *Luke 7* if you want to look at the whole story later. Here's what Jesus said:

Luke 7:40-48 *40 Jesus replied to him, "Simon, I have something to say to you." He said, "Say it, teacher." 41 "A creditor had two debtors. One owed five hundred denarii, and the other fifty. 42 Since they could not pay it back, he graciously forgave them both. So, which of them will love him more?" 43 Simon answered, "I suppose the one he forgave more." "You have judged correctly," he told him. 44 Turning to the woman, he said to Simon, "Do you see this woman? I entered your house; you gave me no water for my feet, but she, with her tears, has washed my feet and wiped them with her hair. 45 You gave me no kiss, but she hasn't stopped kissing my feet since I came in. 46 You didn't anoint my head with olive oil, but she has anointed my feet with perfume. 47 Therefore I tell you, her many sins have been forgiven; that's why she loved much.*

But the one who is forgiven little, loves little." ⁴⁸ Then he said to her, "Your sins are forgiven." (Christian Standard Bible)

I think I can see Bea in that story. I saw Bea as someone who loved Jesus and desired to serve Him because she had been forgiven much.

She was often encouraging after sermons when she would share how the message had impacted her that day. Sometimes she would even share some insight she had gained from another pastor she had listened to and thought it would encourage me too.

Bea loved the Word of God and spent time reading both the Bible and books or devotionals. She would often quote Scripture that applied to something we were talking about or even in a Bible study. She had favorite verses but for the life of me, I cannot recall any she quoted. So... I asked one of her friends and she pointed me to *Psalm 91:1*. I think the first verse alone might miss some of the emphasis, so let me read all of it.

Psalm 91:1-16 *¹ The one who lives under the protection of the Highest dwells in the shadow of the Almighty. ² I will say concerning the Lord, who is my refuge and my fortress, my God in whom I trust: ³ He himself will rescue you from the bird trap, from the destructive plague. ⁴ He will cover you with his feathers; you will take refuge under his wings. His faithfulness will be a protective shield.*

5 You will not fear the terror of the night, the arrow that flies by day, 6 the plague that stalks in darkness, or the pestilence that ravages at noon. 7 Though a thousand fall at your side and ten thousand at your right hand, the pestilence will not reach you. 8 You will only see it with your eyes and witness the punishment of the wicked. 9 Because you have made the Lord my refuge, the Highest your dwelling place, 10 no harm will come to you; no plague will come near your tent. 11 For he will give his angels orders concerning you, to protect you in all your ways. 12 They will support you with their hands so that you will not strike your foot against a stone. 13 You will tread on the lion and the cobra; you will trample the young lion and the serpent. 14 Because he has his heart set on me, I will deliver him; I will protect him because he knows my name. 15 When he calls out to me, I will answer him; I will be with him in trouble. I will rescue him and give him honor. 16 I will satisfy him with a long life and show him my salvation. (Christian Standard Bible)

I can easily see why Bea found strength and encouragement through this Psalm. The last few years of her life were difficult years. Her COPD continued to worsen and the oxygen bottles became a necessary accessory. She became dependent on friends to get her to doctors or treatments. Then not too long ago she discovered that she had cancer. And just last week, the doctors had said there was nothing else they could do. The decline was more rapid than any could imagine.

It seems that on Thursday she was laughing, talking and being Bea and on Saturday she went to be with the Lord.

This Psalm is about protection of the Almighty on those who trust in Him. At first glance, you might question how this Psalm could be true when Bea continued to decline. The evil one likes that line of questioning and doubt it raises and even used verses 11-12 in his temptation of Jesus when trying to get Him to jump off the Temple: *11 For he will give his angels orders concerning you, to protect you in all your ways. 12 They will support you with their hands so that you will not strike your foot against a stone.* Jesus rebuked Satan.

As you know, later Jesus would suffer tremendously on the cross as He took upon Himself the sins of the world. These verses don't guarantee a life free from troubles or even death. What they are, are guarantees of God's presence and protection in and through the struggles. It is His promise that He never leaves us nor forsakes us. I liken them to His promise that we find in *Romans 8:28* that He will work all things to our good if we love Him and are called according to His purpose. He promises divine healing either on this side of heaven or on the other side **in** heaven.

I'm not going to pretend that Bea never got discouraged during her last year. I prayed with her more than once when she was discouraged. It discouraged her when she couldn't come to church. It discouraged her when she couldn't spend time with friends.

She fought to live as long as she could but when the time came to no longer fight, she had confidence that whenever this life would come to an end that there was complete healing in the presence of Jesus in heaven because she had trusted in Jesus Christ as her Lord and Savior.

I don't think Bea would want us to make a lot of her she would want Christ to be exalted. But, I think He is exalted in the demonstration of a life transformed by His grace. I can't leave without this last testimony from Bea's life. Bea had a heart of gold. and she touched many lives for Christ. I don't think she knew that. She had just done what she thought God was leading her to do to be Bea.

Her influence was evidenced on Saturday. While in the bed, struggling to breath and unresponsive, she was surrounded by friends. They sang songs some of the same songs that John has been leading us in today's service. They prayed. They asked God to grant divine healing if it was His will but if not to let her cross from this life to the next without pain or suffering.

They physically touched her by placing a hand on her arm or by holding her hand. They did that even as the last breaths slipped from her mouth. I've never been more proud of them for their demonstration of love and care even until the last second, they never left her alone.

My wife was there and after we were home, she shared with me something that happened as she watched Bea slip from this life to the next. I don't believe she had ever witnessed someone die. I can't do it justice but I'll try to share what she shared with me. Mary was still a little stunned by having just witnessed Bea pass away when she sensed around her a burst of happiness and joy. It wasn't something in her because she was still stunned. She looked around to see if anyone else had felt it. She asked me about it.

I can't explain it, but can, I guess? There is a spiritual world that we cannot see. If we are believers and followers of Jesus, the second we take our last breath here, we take our next breath in heaven. I think Mary may have sensed something from the spiritual world. She sensed that when Bea went from struggling to live here, she went to living in the joyous presence of Jesus in heaven with great happiness with eternal life. I don't know if anyone else in that room experienced it. But what I do know is that Bea went to be with Jesus, and it was the most joyous experience she had ever had.

How do you know that you may ask? It's not because she was a good person, or an encourager, or that she served within the church, or even her influence in the lives of others. It was because there was a time in her life that she faced the truth that she was a sinner separated from a relationship with God. She surrendered her life to Jesus Christ who had died on the cross for her sins, was buried, and was raised on the third day.

The moment she did that her sins were forgiven and she became a child of God who Jesus through the Holy Spirit never quit transforming. The Apostle Paul wrote in his short letter to the Philippians that he had not arrived but was forgetting the past and pressing on to the prize of God's calling.(*Philippians 3:13-14*)

Bea's husband Will had a saying that I've used often to describe that transforming journey "I haven't arrived but I've left."

On Saturday, Bea arrived and she spent her first Sunday in heaven.

If she could speak to us today, there are three things I think she'd say.

1. Don't grieve for me because I'm in a place so beautiful and peaceful that you can't imagine. She would understand our sadness but encourage us to have joy.

2. I want you in heaven with me. If you haven't ever surrendered your life to Jesus Christ and trusted in Him, she would say, "Don't wait. Do it now!"

3. If you love someone, don't wait to tell them. You never know when the opportunity to do that we come to an end. I think Bea took every opportunity to let those in her life know that she loved them.

I want to thank you again for coming to celebrate Bea's life. Let me close in prayer.

Rev. Fred Thompson, Pastor

ACKNOWLEDGEMENTS

Bea, your will to survive, to prove the treatment team wrong, to do the work of recovery and growing in Jesus made your life book worthy.

You became a living testimony to the power of real recovery, a trophy of His grace and a channel of His love.

My family is richly blessed to have known your love and wisdom up close and personal.

May this honor your amazing, overcoming life and continue to hold out your hand of hope to those who still suffer in the clutches of addiction, anxiety, trauma and sin.

Thank you, Lea Yetter, for capturing the love and joy of our friendship in your photo.

Thank you, Renee Corwine, for your editing.

Thank you, Cara Quarantillo, for your patience in cover design for our rainbow girl.

ABOUT THE AUTHOR

In addition to serving as Vice President of the Behavioral Health Network for WellSpan Health, Dr. Shannon Terrell Gordon devotes time as a researcher, author, speaker and teacher. She works to document stories of resilience, to develop tools help each person live their best and most meaningful life.

REVIEW ASK PAGE

It would help continue sharing Bea's amazing story if you would go to Amazon to leave your honest review.

*Would you **please?***

Made in the USA
Columbia, SC
12 April 2024

34292097R00157